angels

and you

DISCERNING THE PRESENCE
AND ACTIVITY OF ANGELS

Graeme **Wylie**

Published by
Maurice Wylie Media
Inspirational Christian Publisher

Publishers' statement: Throughout this book the love for our God is such that whenever we refer to Him, we honour with Capitals. On the other hand, when referring to the devil, we refuse to acknowledge him with any honour to the point of violating grammatical rule and withholding capitalisation.

For more information visit
www.MauriceWylieMedia.com

Dedication

I would like to dedicate this book to the memory of my late friend, intercessor and true prophet, Noel McKinney.

Acknowledgements

I would like to give grateful thanks to Judith Ferraro, Robert Holden, and my wife Frances for proofreading the original draft, and for making corrections and helpful suggestions for the improvement of the text. I would also like to thank those who encouraged me to write, including many who brought me prophetic words to that end, especially Rosemary McAuley who gave me a pen as a prophetic gift at my commissioning as a missionary to France.

Contents

Foreword

From early on in my life, I have always been fascinated by angels and the angelic realm.

It is amazing how often they show up throughout the Scriptures and, while one doesn't want to highlight them over the glory of God, it is plain to see in Scripture that they exist to do just that, to promote the glory of God.

I was really excited a couple of years back when my good friend Graeme Wylie sent me a copy of his book *Angels in our Territory*. I knew Graeme and Fran to be a couple who blazed a trail in Ireland for the cause of Christ. I knew they never shied away from the tough grind of ministry and their stickability always impressed me. I have to say I wondered what Graeme had to say about angels. With Fran being an instrument of prophetic guidance for us in Emmanuel over the years, let's say when the book arrived, I knew I needed to read this book pronto and I was not disappointed.

Over the years I personally have had several encounters which have been quite profound. And this book, *Angels in our Territory* was exactly that, profound, and a very biblical view of our heavenly messengers.

I wondered where Graeme got this material and thought, ah, I know! You see, Graeme is a man of the Word and of prayer. When you mix those two things together with a lifetime of dedication and devotion to the work of the Lord the result is, revelation and insight into Kingdom things. And now here we are with book two, *Angels and You*.

This new book is a mixture of all that I have already said about Graeme, insight and revelation. Again, I devoured the script that he had sent me. His honesty and vulnerability along with his delicate handling of a subject that some writers have decimated in times past, impressed and blessed me so much. The angelic and human partnership has always intrigued me since I was a boy, yet I have been aware that some writers and books have taught faulty doctrines which took the whole subject of angels off on a tangent.

Graeme handles this so well, showing powerfully the many roles they have and the things we can miss so easily. How when God gives us an assignment, he also assigns angels to be with us and to serve us on that assignment. How they war for us and stand with us, bring joy and inspire huge measures of faith. As I read the script I declared in my soul, it is definitely so good to know that there are more for us and with us than there are against us.

Maybe you're like me and have wondered about angels showing up with Daniel in the den of lions, or Jacob's vision with the angels ascending and descending a ladder. Or maybe about Abraham's three friends who visited for tea, or maybe even the two named ones, Michael and Gabriel. Or Peter's miraculous release from prison or Paul's encounter in the middle of a pending shipwreck. Or even Jesus himself in the loneliest times of His earthly journey, the wilderness and Gethsemane. If these are your ponderings, then this book is for you.

Preachers will use this book when preaching on angels (I know I will). Small group leaders will use it in small group studies, how do I know this? Because I know Graeme, and I know this book is born out of a lifetime of service but also countless hours, weeks and years of study. And of course, obedience to the call of God to write it. So you are in for a treat. I feel privileged to have got reading it before you! So, personally I'd like to say, 'thank you Graeme for sharing such wisdom and truth' and to the rest of you, 'sit back, grab a fresh cuppa and get yourself into this feast of writings.'

Philip Emerson
Lead pastor Emmanuel Church, Lurgan, Northern Ireland.

Preface

When angels show up in Scripture they usually appear in a way that people can see them with their natural eyes. They may appear in human form and may not be recognised as angels. Or they may appear as glorious, luminous, or powerful fiery beings which are overwhelming to the human eye. These appearances are usually unexpected and unsought. And there are a lot of them throughout both Old and New Testaments.

Like many Christians, I grew up with an awareness of these biblical angelic appearances, but I never expected that I would ever see an angel or collaborate with angels in ministry. I was conditioned to think that if God wanted to send an angel to me, he would do so sovereignly, when and if he wanted to. It would be independent of any activity or expectation on my part. And if he were to send them I would see them, hear them or in some way be physically aware of them.

The only exception to this in my thinking was the activity of guardian angels whom I firmly believed to be in operation invisibly around all those who fear the Lord. But, on reflection, why should invisible angelic ministry be limited to their protective role? To restrict other angelic spheres of service to happening in the visible realm is to severely limit the provision God has made for his invisible ministering spirits to serve us in all kinds of ways.

Scripture is clear that angels are present with us to serve us and to collaborate with us in a whole range of functions. Yet we either ignore or are largely unaware of their presence and activity in our favour. Hebrews 1:14 tells us that they are ministering spirits sent to serve us as we carry out the assignments that God has given us in life.

Scripture clearly teaches that angels are essentially spirit beings. They are 'ministering spirits'. While they may and do still manifest in various physical forms, essentially as spirit beings they are normally invisible to the human eye. We usually find it easier to acknowledge the invisible presence of the Holy Spirit just because he is uniquely spirit and does not usually manifest his presence in a physical form, as angels may do. The one clear exception to this is when the Holy Spirit manifested in the form of a dove at the baptism of Jesus. It was not a dove but the Holy Spirit manifesting in the form or appearance of a dove, just as satan manifested in the form of a serpent in the Garden of Eden. But that is not how the Holy Spirit or satan normally operate. So, usually we have less difficulty in being aware of their invisible presence and activity, helping or hindering us in our lives.

Just because angels in Scripture more frequently manifest in some visible or audible way does not alter the basic fact that they are essentially spirit beings. Hebrew 1:7 'In speaking of the angels he says, 'He makes his angels spirits, and his servants flames of fire.' As spirit beings, they are normally invisible to our natural eyes but nevertheless they are constantly on assignment, sent by God to help and serve us, particularly in entering into the fullness of our inheritance and ministry. Hebrews 1:14 'Are not all angels ministering spirits sent to serve those who will inherit salvation?' Exodus 23:20 'See, I am sending an angel ahead of you to guard you along the way and to bring you to the place I have prepared.' Personally speaking, a new understanding and experience of these verses has brought a powerful new awareness to our life and ministry in recent years.

Dutch Sheets in his book 'Angel Armies' says 'Wake up to angelic activity!' It brings a turnaround in many situations today just as for Peter and Paul and all the apostles. It shapes the way we live and face difficulties. It equips us for spiritual warfare. It transforms the way we do ministry. We tune in to the spirit realm. We ask God to give us discernment of what is going on in that realm. Jesus only did what he saw the Father doing. We can ask God for discernment to become aware of the angels the Father is sending to help us, and what their particular assignment is. Then we can collaborate with them on that assignment.

In my experience, angels don't usually force their way into our consciousness. We tune in to the spirit realm in which they operate. We ask God to open our spiritual eyes as Elisha did for his servant. Neither of them saw God's protective angelic army around them with their natural eyes. Elisha saw them with his spiritual eyes and was able to function in faith and without fear. Meanwhile his servant was terrified, until his spiritual eyes were opened.

This is a season when we are learning to co-operate with God the Holy Spirit, as his co-workers, and to co-operate with the angels he sends to work with us. We need our spiritual senses sharpened through exercise and practice so that we are equipped to serve God more effectively. Those who serve the forces of darkness are becoming more sensitised to their spiritual and occult masters. But light is stronger than darkness. It is high time for us to wake up to the angelic realm and live as sons of the light.

In '*Angels and You*' we are, of course talking about the angels of God. Scripture makes clear that Satan has his angels too, and that they often masquerade as angels of light in order to deceive. It seems to me that much of the church has avoided the topic of angels out of fear of people giving them too much importance. But, in failing to give clear teaching, the church has left a vacuum regarding the genuine nature of angelic ministry. Nature hates a vacuum, and the spurious can often fill the space that should be occupied by the authentic. This book is designed to give a solid biblical teaching backed up by authentic experience.

As you read these pages, may God enlighten your understanding and increase your experience of angelic help and ministry too!

Introduction

There is a seismic shift in the spirit realm. We are entering a new season in the outworking of God's purposes. In this season God is increasing awareness of the presence and activity of angels. We have been in a season of preparation long enough; now we are entering into a season of fulfilment. The prophetic words that have been spoken over you, over others, and over nations for many years will converge together in a season of accomplishment. The prophetic streams and tributaries will begin to flow together in a great river of prophetic fulfilment as we move towards the culmination of God's purposes for the earth.

In these days God will pour out His Spirit in greater ways, and as He comes upon us more powerfully, there will be a deeper awakening of all our spiritual faculties that will bring us to a place of greater spiritual alertness. In this state of heightened spiritual sensitivity, we will be able to pick up on our spiritual antennae the things that God has for us in this time. This will include a greater awareness of the presence and activity of angels.

God operates on planet earth through his servants. He has two contingents of servants – his children and his angels. He has assigned the work of evangelism and discipling the nations to us, the Church. And He has assigned the ministry of helping us to our fellow-servants, the angels. Our life and ministry has changed since coming into this understanding of 'partnering with angels.

So we will look at the Scriptures which teach us how God works through his servants, the angels, and how we can partner with them, so that we may be more fully equipped and prepared for every good work which God has planned for us in this season.

Are you ready?

Graeme Wylie

"When we obey, in the spirit realm angels are activated."

CHAPTER 1

When an Angel shows up

We had just returned home after a few days away on a rather spiritually demanding assignment when an angel came and sat beside Fran, my wife. I had gone out at the time and she was feeling quite overwhelmed by the assignment we had just undertaken.

Three years previously God had spoken to me during a visit to France and said, 'Stay in this land for a season, the land of Occitanie.' At the time we were in the region then known as the Languedoc. So we began to make plans to relocate as soon as we could hand over our existing responsibilities, and two years later we moved to the Languedoc. The following year the French government decided to restructure the administrative regions of the country. Languedoc was merged with the larger region of Midi-Pyrenées and the new enlarged region was eventually renamed 'Occitanie,' the name God had spoken to me about three years previously![1]

This caught my attention and as I began to seek God about it he made it clear to me that this larger region was, in fact, the territory God had assigned to us. Our assignment from God was to travel throughout Occitanie praying for the territory and its people and asking God to send revival to this region. Geographically it was approximately the same size as Ireland with a similar population. Having spent nearly forty years in Ireland, mainly in the Connacht region, this seemed a much bigger assignment.

---

[1]   For a fuller account see my book 'Angels in our Territory'

We began to travel throughout Occitanie praying continually as we went. At times there was a deep spirit of intercession that laid hold of us as we cried out to God to pour out his Spirit. At times there was a real heaviness and it felt like we were wading through spiritual treacle. At times we sang and worshipped, aware of the angels accompanying us. At one place, near the Cevennes, we felt like Jacob at Bethel, that we were on holy ground and there were angels all around, a veritable gate of heaven. There was such an awesome sense of the presence of God. I fell on my face on the ground and kicked off my shoes. Meantime, Fran was dancing and singing with the joy of God's presence. (The Cevennes is a region where there was a powerful prophetic revival in the seventeenth century among the Huguenots).

On one occasion, returning home from the border with Andorra, we experienced an oppressive sense of spiritual darkness. It was at this stage that Fran began to feel quite overwhelmed. When she asked God to help her to feel for the people in need in the area she began to weep. She felt so overwhelmed by the greatness of the need and our smallness in contrast. She wept and wept as we travelled along.

When we got home I had to go out for an appointment, and Fran went to sit in the front garden, still feeling so overwhelmed and weak facing our assignment. It was then that an angel came and sat beside her. She could not see him but he spoke to her and said, *Your weakness is a treasure, because when you are weak I am detailed to help you.* This direct message delivered by the angel had a remarkable and strengthening effect on her and continues to do so. Could it be that Paul had had a similar experience when he said, *When I am weak then I am strong?* [2]

The angel continued to say to Fran, *Be encouraged. When you are weak, we are strong on your behalf. And we, (including you) therefore, have at our back all the resources of heaven.* Fran then asked the angel about what we had done in weakness in the places we had gone to pray. He replied, *We were already there. We were there ahead of you because we*

---

2   2 Corinthians 12:10

knew you were coming. We always go ahead because of God's word to you. When we first went to France God had given us the word, *See, I am sending an angel ahead of you to guard you along the way and to bring you to the place I have prepared.³*

Through this experience Fran became aware that we had been assigned a mighty angel and that he was not alone; he had others with him. When we go in obedience to God's command, the angels are aware of our assignment and go ahead of us to prepare the way. What a wonderful knowledge to have when God gives us challenging assignments!

The key for all of us is to find God's assignment for our life. We had taken time to fast and pray and seek the Lord as I was approaching retirement age, to know what God had for us in the next season. I had said to God '*You are my Lord and you have the right to direct my life. You have the right to send us anywhere in the world, into any situation of need or any situation of danger that You want. I want to be just as available to You at this stage in life as I was as a young man forty years ago.*' At that stage I set off overseas on mission with my suitcase and sleeping bag, even going behind the 'Iron Curtain' to bring in bibles when it was dangerous to do so.

But our assignment could be in our home, our work, our neighbourhood or just to love one other person with the love of the Lord. As we do what God has assigned us to do, then He has angels to help and serve us in that assignment. They go ahead of us to prepare the way and they guard us and strengthen us on the way. Angels are messengers who deliver God's messages to us.

Now, isn't that amazing to know that when God gives us assignments, an angel is assigned to help us to fulfil God's will?

---

3   Exodus 23:20

What do we learn from all this?

Firstly, angels are an integral part of God's ways of working.

Secondly, when God gives us an assignment, he also assigns angels to be with us and to serve us on that assignment.

Thirdly, a feeling of weakness should not hold us back from obeying God's assignments since heaven's resources are at our disposal. We just need to call on them!

CHAPTER 2

Who or what are Angels?

One of the clearest verses of Scripture regarding the nature and ministry of angels is Hebrews 1:14. *'Are not all angels ministering spirits sent to serve those who will inherit salvation?'* They are described as **ministering spirits.** They are spirit beings as opposed to physical beings. God is Spirit, (John 4:24) that means He is not housed in a body like we are. He exists as a pure Spirit Being who possesses a personality but not a body.

In His incarnation Jesus, the Son of Father God, took a human body in order to become a man so that He could draw an alienated mankind back to God. Man is also essentially a spirit being, since he is made in the image of God. He also has a personality, comprising mind, will and emotions, just like God. But unlike God he lives in a body.

God is described as *the Father of spirits* (Hebrews 12:9) and *the Father from whom every family in heaven and earth derives its name.* (Ephesians 3:15) God created a human family for whom He is Father, and in heaven He has created the angels, for whom He is also Father. Some of these angels are specifically referred to as 'the sons of God.' They are part of the created order in the invisible realm. They were created before the material creation and rejoiced when God created the earth. (Job 38:4-7)

Many people in the world find it difficult to accept that there is a God, never mind an invisible God. But have you considered the clothes that are hung out to dry on a clothesline when the wind is blowing? Just because you cannot see the wind does not mean there is no wind; the effects of it are there. Likewise, the effects of our God exist in the beauty of our planet, galaxy etc – even you and me! Scripture shows us that God is like the wind (John 3:8), Like the wind He is invisible to human eyes.

*'The Son is the image of the **invisible God**, the firstborn over all creation. For in him all things were created: things in heaven and on earth, **visible and invisible**, whether thrones or **powers or rulers or authorities**; all things have been created through him and for him.'* Colossians 1:15-16

The angels are also part of this invisible creation. They exist as a hierarchy with governmental ranks, each having various levels of power and jurisdiction. There are **cherubim** and **seraphim**, **angels** and **archangels**. They exist in a parallel dimension alongside our own visible world.

They interact with our world, as we see frequently throughout Scripture, both in the Old Testament and the New Testament. At times they appear as glorious beings before whom humans fall down overpowered by their awesome appearance. (Daniel 10:5-9) At other times they take human form and look just like men. (Genesis 18:1-2,16; 19:1) Sometimes they appear and other times they are not seen at all, but they speak and act on God's behalf.

Angels can appear and disappear in a flash. The angel that announced Samson's birth to his parents appeared as a man, albeit an awesome man. Manoah, Samson's father, didn't initially realise that he was an angel at all. When Manoah made a sacrifice to God and lit a fire on the altar, the angel of the Lord ascended in the flame and disappeared! (Judges 13:6-13) That's when Manoah realised that he had in fact been visited by an angel.

This angel had announced to them the assignment God was giving them for the rest of their lives – to birth, bring up, and nurture the next anointed leader for their nation. They had found their life's mission through the surprise visit of an angel to give them directions in how to carry it out. Parenting is an awesome assignment from God that truly needs God's wisdom and grace. Angels are available to carry God's messages to us and to help us in that assignment.

The references to cherubim and seraphim describe the **cherubim as having two, four or six wings and the seraphim as having six wings and flying.** Other lesser ranks of messenger angels are not said to have wings, though Daniel does mention that the angel Gabriel, who appeared to him as a man, came to him in 'swift flight.' (Daniel 9:21) In none of the other references to them in human form does it mention them as having wings. They just appear and disappear. A spiritual being does not have to have wings to move.

Daniel was accustomed to angelic activity, but when he was thrown in the lions' den he does not mention seeing angels protecting him in the den. But when the king asked Daniel if his God had been able to save him from the lions, Daniel replied, *'My **God sent his angel**, and he shut the mouths of the lions.'* Daniel 6:21

Likewise, when Abraham sent his servant to find a wife for Isaac, Abraham assured his hesitant servant, *'The Lord, the God of heaven, who brought me out of my father's household and my native land and who spoke to me and promised me on oath, saying, "To your offspring I will give this land"– **he will send his angel before you** so that you can get a wife for my son from there.'* Genesis 24:7

There is no record of the angel appearing in the story that unfolds, but the miraculous answer to the servant's prayer regarding Rebekah clearly demonstrates divine activity in operation.

In my experience to date, I have discerned in my spirit the presence
and activity of angels rather than seeing them with my physical eyes,
although both are possible. The nature of the gift of 'discerning of
spirits' (1 Corinthians 12:10) is that it operates at the level of the
human spirit in interaction with the Holy Spirit, rather than at
the level of the physical. In the case of my wife, referred to in the
introduction, she discerned that it was an angel that sat beside her
and began speaking to her.

God wants us to be more conscious of this unseen realm of the spirit
world and to be aware of the roles and functions God has ordained
for them on our behalf.

Jesus is far superior to the angels

Most of Hebrews chapter one is devoted to outlining the superiority
of Jesus over the angels. This is important for us to bear in mind. It is
possible for us to be too focused on angels and talking so much about
angels that we get the angelic realm out of perspective. So before
giving us the important verse fourteen, which outlines the ministry
of angels for us, the writer to the Hebrews, gives us most of a chapter
talking about the superiority of Jesus. He gives us at least ten ways in
which Jesus is superior to angels.

The Son
The first reason given is the uniqueness of Jesus' Sonship. The angels
may be sons of God in the sense that they were created by Him as
the Father of creation, but Jesus is in a unique relationship with the
Father. He is of the same genus as the Father, of the 'same substance.'[4]
He is divine.

God
In many English versions of the Bible Jesus is often referred to as
the 'only begotten Son of God.'[5] The Greek original is *'monogenes'*.

---

4   *Greek homoousios. Nicene creed*
5   *John 1:14,18;3:16,18*

It was translated 'only begotten' because it was thought that it came from two Greek words *'mono'* (only) and *'gennao'* (to beget, bear). More recently Greek scholars believe that the second part of the word comes from *'genos'* (kind, class).[6] So instead of meaning 'only begotten', *'monogenes'* means 'unique, one of a kind'. Angels are not of the same *'genos'* as Jesus. He is uniquely superior to them.

Worshipped

Jesus is to be worshipped by the angels, but the angels are not to be worshipped at all.

'And again, when God brings his firstborn into the world, he says, "Let all God's angels worship him."" Hebrews 1:6

This shows the clearest distinction between the position of Jesus as God in contrast to the angels, who are created beings.

No matter what rank of angel they are, each one is called to worship Jesus. None is exempt. He is to be worshipped because He is God. None of them are remotely on or near His level. When John the apostle fell at an angel's feet to worship him, the angel told him,

'Don't do that! I am a fellow servant with you and with your brothers and sisters who hold to the testimony of Jesus.' Revelation 19:10

We, as humans, like to receive praise and acclamation from others but Jesus taught that seeking the praise of men is an expression of pride and is a blockage to faith. (John 5:44) The angels know that they are not to receive worship from humans. The pride of seeking worship was the source of Lucifer's downfall and his demonic followers still seek worship. But the angels of God do not. They consider themselves to be our fellow servants who worship God alone.

Most of us reading this book will be familiar with the scene of the

---

6   The Unseen Realm, Michael Heiser.

angel appearing to the shepherds to announce the birth of the Saviour. We are used to nativity scenes with a few children dressed up as angels singing *Glory to God in the highest and on earth peace.*

But Luke records a breath-taking scene that we have often failed to capture:

*'Suddenly **a great company of the heavenly host** appeared with the angel, praising God and saying, "Glory to God in the highest heaven, and on earth peace to those on whom his favour rests.'* Luke 2:13-14

When God brought his Son into the world, according to the original Greek, He summoned all the angels to worship His Son.

The Greek word which is variously translated as 'a great company' or 'multitude' is the word *'plethos.'* According to Thayer[7] this refers to 'the whole number' or 'the whole multitude of angels.'

According to Strong[8] it means 'the fullness'. It is used to refer to the full complement or the complete crew of a ship. **Thus the full complement of heaven's angel armies filled the skies over Bethlehem as God the Father summoned them to worship his Son and welcome him into the world!** The earth resounded to the strains of this angelic choir as it sang God's praises and announced God's 'Shalom' to those on earth for whom his grace and favour had just arrived in the form of this newborn babe who was God incarnate, God with us. Let all God's angels worship him! And they all continue to do so.

Lord
*'In writing of the angels he says, "He makes his angels spirits, and his **servants** flames of fire.'* Hebrews 1:7

---

7   *Thayer Bible Dictionary free download*
8   *Strong's Exhaustive Concordance on line*

This is a reaffirmation of the nature of their existence – they are spirit-beings – and the purpose of their existence – to be God's servants. So by their very nature and function they are inferior to Jesus.

Philippians 2:9-11 says, *'Therefore God exalted him to the highest place and gave him the name that is above every name, that at the name of Jesus every knee should bow, in heaven and on earth and under the earth, and every tongue acknowledge that Jesus Christ is Lord, to the glory of God the Father.'*

As servants, the angels are subject to the authority of Jesus who is Lord of all.

God
Hebrews proceeds to contrast Jesus, the King of the universe, to the angels, his subjects.

'But about the Son he says, "Your throne, O God, will last for ever and ever; a sceptre of justice will be the sceptre of your kingdom.' Hebrews 1:8

You can clearly see in that verse Jesus is addressed as God. He reigns on the throne of the universe as God and King. His kingdom is an eternal kingdom and He will reign for ever and ever. As a king He will wield a sceptre which represents his executive authority to do what he decrees.

Perfect justice will be the hallmark of God's eternal kingdom. What an exalted state Jesus occupies! No higher place exists in the entire universe. By contrast, the angels are His servants listening for His Word and always willing to obey His orders and execute His decrees.

*'Praise the Lord, **you his angels, you mighty ones who do his bidding**, who obey his word. Praise the Lord, all his heavenly hosts, **you his servants who do his will.'*** Psalms 103:20-21

Highest place

The writer to the Hebrews was evidently addressing a contemporary danger: a heretical tendency to give the angels too exalted a position in their thinking. Some even went as far as to worship angels as perceived intermediaries between man and God. Paul warned about this danger too.

'Do not let anyone who delights in false humility and the worship of angels disqualify you. Such a person also goes into great detail about what they have seen; they are puffed up with idle notions by their unspiritual mind.' Colossians 2:18

So, to ensure that we keep angels in the proper place in our thinking and theology, Hebrews makes point after point to emphasise the supremacy and uniqueness of Jesus in contrast to the angels.

He continues by asserting that God has set Jesus above His companions, (Hebrews 1:9) possibly referring to the other sons of God, the angels. Furthermore, Jesus is the Creator who laid the foundations of the earth and fashioned the heavens. (Hebrews 1:10)

He is eternal and immutable (Hebrews 1:11-12), two attributes of deity that angels do not possess. Finally, He asks the question:

'To which of the angels did God ever say, Sit at my right hand until I make your enemies a footstool for your feet?'

Jesus has been accorded the highest place in heaven, the place of ultimate authority, at the Father's right hand. No angel comes remotely near. Paul also makes clear that God has seated Christ *at his right hand in the heavenly realms,* **far above all rule and authority, power and dominion, and every name that is invoked,** *not only in the present age but also in the one to come.' Ephesians 1:20-21*

So, on all these counts Jesus is unique and far superior to the angels and the One on whom we are to keep our eyes fixed. (Hebrew 12:2)

A Note of Caution

We are, of course, talking about the angels of God, not the fallen angels of satan. (Revelation 12:7)

The hordes of satan are in active rebellion against God, and, like satan, their leader, they operate by trying to deceive humans by posing as good angels. Paul warned us *that satan himself masquerades as an angel of light.'* 2 Corinthians 11:14

In people's search for spirituality they are often drawn into a counterfeit spirituality through New Age deceptions which lead them away from the truth into experience-based delusions. Beware of the proliferation of 'angel' paraphernalia such as 'angel cards' and the like which are found in 'angel shops.' Make sure that all 'spiritual experience' is checked out against Scripture which is our only sure guide to that which is good and holy.

One of our friends got deceived by such charlatans who led her into 'spiritual experiences' in which she was led by 'angel guides' and astral travel into some other-worldly experiences.

It sounded wonderful at the beginning, but in the end, she came to us for help as she felt she was going out of her mind. She had to be set free from these spiritual beings that had begun to take her over and torment her. Thank God she was set free and has since been grateful for the greater liberating reality of the Holy Spirit.

CHAPTER 3

God's servants, His Angels

Many people think of angels primarily as guardians who exercise a protective role. That is, of course, an important function that they have, and we will examine that in more detail later. But not all angels are guardian angels. Their ministry is much more comprehensive and has two major aspects: firstly, their ministry to God, whose servants they are, and secondly, angelic ministry to us as heirs of God's great salvation.

Their most fundamental role is that of service. *'Are not all angels ministering spirits sent to serve those who will inherit salvation?'* Hebrews 1:14

They are God's servants who are sent to serve mankind in God's great plan of salvation. They are his agents to execute His plans and carry out His will on earth. He has two cohorts operating on His behalf on the earth, **two sets of servants: the angels and the Church.**

The Greek word translated ministering in this verse is *'leitourgikos.'* According to Thayer[9] it means 'relating to the performance of service, employed in ministering.' It is ministry performed by a *'leitourgos'*, who, according to Thayer[10] is 'a public minister, a servant of the state.'

In the contemporary Greek world of the New Testament era it was used of three specific areas of service:

---

9   Thayer op. cit.
10   Ibid

Priestly service
Royal service
Military service

It referred to the service offered in the pagan temples by the priests with various acts of worship and homage, or in the royal court by the king's attendants, who waited on the king and were sent on missions by the king. It was also used to refer to service in the state army in the various ranks.

When we study the ministry of angels in Scripture it also falls into these three areas of service, as, indeed, does ours.

Priestly service

The primary function of the angels is the priestly service of worship. In the Book of Revelation, the veil obscuring the heavenly realm is pulled back and we are given a glimpse of the angelic worship which goes on continually in heaven.

'Then I looked and heard the voice of many angels, numbering thousands upon thousands, and ten thousand times ten thousand. They encircled the throne and the living creatures and the elders. In a loud voice they were saying: 'Worthy is the Lamb, who was slain, to receive power and wealth and wisdom and strength and honour and glory and praise!' Revelation 5:11-12

There are millions of angels continually engaged in worship to God and bowing before Him in adoration in heaven. The atmosphere is one of joy and celebration, can you wait to get there? And every time a sinner repents, the angels rejoice, so that means a lot of joy and celebration in heaven as millions of people from around the world come to faith in Christ every year.

'I tell you, there is rejoicing in the presence of the angels of God over one sinner who repents.' Luke 15:10

It reminds me of the 'France en Feu' conference in Paris. I was standing by the door when a young child of about seven or eight entered with her mother. When she heard the music and singing and saw the dancing and banner waving and sensed the atmosphere, her eyes lit up and she exclaimed excitedly to her mother, 'It's a party!'

The angels and saints in heaven are not having a dull time so why should we? And as we bring our worship to God we are seen in Scripture as joining a joyful angelic celebration.

*'But **you have come** to Mount Zion, to the city of the living God, the heavenly Jerusalem. **You have come** to thousands upon thousands of **angels in joyful assembly,** to the church of the firstborn, whose names are written in heaven.'* Hebrews 12:22-23

When the Spirit leads our worship and we bring our human spirits into the presence of God, we join the angels in their joyful assembly. Suddenly we can become aware of the angels present with us. We discern their presence as they release the atmosphere of heaven, the atmosphere has gone up a notch and a new level of joy is released.

As we respond to the Spirit, we are brought into more intimate encounters with the Lord.

On one hand the angels respond to our praise and celebration. They serve in the presence of God and are attracted to people who are worshipping God in Spirit and truth. They come to join in our worship. We, in turn, respond to their presence and raise our level of worship and praise. Sometimes angels' voices join with ours and the volume of worship rises. Sometimes the musicians hear the angels playing musical instruments and are inspired to reproduce those heavenly sounds, even playing chords and sounds they have never played before! Truly Spirit-inspired, heavenly worship!

The angels serve to connect heaven and earth, to bring heaven to earth and the presence of God to his people. We see this in Jacob's dream, where he saw a ladder reaching from earth to heaven. God was standing at the top of the ladder, waiting to speak to Jacob and angels were ascending and descending on the ladder. (Genesis 28:12-13) Then God spoke and revealed himself to Jacob, giving him wonderful promises about the journey he was undertaking and his future destiny. Jacob responded by saying,

'How awesome is this place! This is none other than the house of God; this is the gate of heaven.' Genesis 28:17

We want our church gatherings to be true encounters with the living God who reveals himself to us and speaks to us.

We see in Genesis 28 that angels are pictured as ascending and descending on the ladder connecting heaven and earth. They transmit the sense of the presence of God and bring us to the gate of heaven. This interface between heaven and earth Jacob experienced in a dual sense. It was God's house on earth, so he named the earthly place Bethel, meaning 'house of God.' But it was also the 'gate of heaven;' he had been transported into the heavenly realms. Others in Scripture experience this as well…

John the Apostle, in Revelation 4:1, is transported into the heavenly realms. He hears a voice saying, *'Come up here!'* He is transported in the Spirit into the heavenly realms where he sees the heavenly scene of angelic worship around the throne of God. That invitation is being heard by the Church around the world in these days, *Come up here!* The question is: are we listening? Are we responding to that invitation?

Some churches are now more set up for entertainment and those born of the Spirit are increasingly disappointed with these forms of worship that do not usher us into the presence of God. Church must be centred around His presence.

Those born of the Spirit are increasingly responding to the voice of the Spirit and we bring our spirits into the heavenly realms to join our worship with the worship of the angels around the throne.

The angel who was giving John a guided tour around the heavenly realms described himself as '...*I am a fellow servant with you and with your brothers and sisters who hold to the testimony of Jesus. Worship God!*' Revelation 19:10

The angels see themselves as our fellow servants in this priestly service of praise and worship to our common Lord and King.

A place of priestly service

In Israel's earthly tabernacle the golden altar was positioned just before the veil, behind which was the Holy of Holies, the inner sanctuary. It was where the Levitical priests burned incense as they offered up prayers to God for the people. It represents the place where we, as new covenant priests in the order of Melchizedek, perform our priestly ministry of worship and intercession.

In heaven, the golden altar is the place where the angels exercise their priestly ministry alongside ours.

'Another angel, who had a golden censer, came and stood at the altar. He was given **much incense** *to offer, with the prayers of all God's people, on the* **golden altar** *in front of the throne. The smoke of the incense, together* **with the prayers of God's people**, *went up before God from the angel's hand. Then the angel took the censer, filled it with fire from the altar,*

*and **hurled it on the earth**; and there came peals of thunder, rumblings, flashes of lightning and an earthquake.'* Revelation 8:3-5

Incense is a perfume that smells sweet and pleasing to the Lord. It is a symbol of the prayer and worship that He loves to receive from us. The angel adds much incense to our prayers which then ascend before God from the angel's hand. So the priestly ministry at the golden altar is a collaborative one between us and the ministering angel who presents our prayers to God. He then takes the golden censer and fills it with fire from the altar and hurls it to the earth.

This means that the angel releases the earthly consequences of our prayers, symbolised by earth-shaking events such as thunder, lightning and earthquakes. Angels offer their priestly service to God in heaven, but the consequences are felt on the earth. We usually think of answered prayer as coming directly from God Himself. It is true that He is the Author but angels are often the means of delivering those answers. For example, in Scripture King Solomon is credited with building the temple at Jerusalem, but it was not Solomon who put those huge stones one on top of the other. It was the workmen, his servants. Similarly God, as King of the universe does His work through His servants the angels, including the delivery of answers to our prayers.

God has given our priestly ministry of worship and intercession a central place in heaven. This declares how important it is in God's eyes as a means of extending God's kingdom on earth.

*'And when he had taken it (the scroll), the four living creatures and the twenty-four elders fell down before the Lamb. Each one had a harp and they were holding **golden bowls full of incense, which are the prayers of God's people.** And they sang a new song, saying: You are worthy to take the scroll and to open its seals, because you were slain, and with your blood you purchased for God persons from every tribe and language and people and nation. You have made them to be a **kingdom and priests** to serve our God, and they will reign on the earth.'* Revelation 5:8-10

In John's vision of heaven, he sees the Lamb standing in the centre of the throne encircled by the four living creatures and twenty-four elders each of whom has a harp and golden bowls full of incense. The description of the four living creatures in Revelation 4 resembles the description of the cherubim in Ezekiel. (Ezekiel 1:5, 10, 14.)

They are glorious creatures associated with the intimate presence of God and the glory of God. Two cherubim made of beaten gold stretched their wings over the mercy seat in the tabernacle and covered the Shekinah glory that appeared over the mercy seat.

The twenty-four elders probably represent the whole people of God from the Old Covenant era and the New Covenant era, symbolized by the twelve tribes of Israel and the twelve apostles of the Lamb.

They each have a harp and are singing a new song of praise to the Lamb. This song is about His blood which He shed as the purchase price for a multi-ethnic, multilingual, multinational people to be a kingdom and priests to serve God and reign on the earth.

This priestly reign is brought about by the priestly intercession and worship as represented by the golden bowls full of incense, which are the prayers of God's holy people. It takes place at the golden altar as we have just seen. It is God's means of bringing about his reign on earth. Heaven impacts earth through this priestly ministry in collaboration with the angels. Our prayers have a mighty impact on earth.

The central prayer Jesus taught us to pray is key: *'Your kingdom come; your will be done on earth as it is in heaven.'* (Matthew 6:10) Like angels, we are called to minister to the Lord. The leaders of the early church in Acts 6, made this their regular practice...

*'While they were **worshipping** the Lord and fasting, the Holy Spirit said, "Set apart for me Barnabas and Saul for the work to which I have called them.'* Acts 13:2

The Greek word translated 'worshipping' in the New International Bible is *'leitourgeo'*, which means 'serving' or 'ministering' and is the same word used in Hebrews 1:14 to refer to the priestly ministry of angels towards the Lord They set us an example in how to minister to the Lord.

What about unanswered prayer?

There are many prayers from wrong motives which we can expect not to be answered. They may be purely selfish, or they may be prayed with good intentions but are not aligned to God's will which we can expect not to be answered. But I'm talking about prayers prayed in faith in God's promises, truly believing specific words He has given us. And yet it seems that many of them are not answered, at least not in the way that we expected, or not within our time-space world. Are those prayers in the golden bowls in heaven? Are they offered up with much incense by the angels too?

The subject of unanswered prayer is a big one, and many books on prayer attempt to address the issue honestly. For me, I am only going to make a few brief comments based on Hebrews 11, the chapter of faith…

The chapter begins by giving us some basic teaching about faith then proceeds to give us many examples of faith in the lives of biblical characters.

'Now faith is confidence in what we hope for and assurance about what we do not see. This is what the ancients were commended for.' v2

'And without faith it is impossible to please God, because anyone who comes to him must believe that he exists and that he rewards those who earnestly seek him.' v6

The next section of the chapter lists the great exploits of faith by Abraham, Moses, Joshua, etc. This is the section that we hear preached most often. It concludes with, '*And what more shall I say? I do not have time to tell about Gideon, Barak, Samson and Jephthah, about David and Samuel and the prophets who through faith conquered kingdoms, administered justice, and gained what was promised; who shut the mouths of lions, quenched the fury of the flames, and escaped the edge of the sword; whose weakness was turned to strength; and who became powerful in battle and routed foreign armies. Women received back their dead, raised to life again.*' v32-35

A huge catalogue of the fantastic accomplishments of faith would you not say! But it doesn't finish there. It continues: '*There were others who were tortured, refusing to be released so that they might gain an even better resurrection. Some faced jeers and flogging, and even chains and imprisonment. They were put to death by stoning; they were sawn in two; they were killed by the sword. They went about in sheepskins and goatskins, destitute, persecuted and ill-treated – the world was not worthy of them. They wandered in deserts and mountains, living in caves and in holes in the ground.*' v35-38

'***These were all commended for their faith***, *yet none of them received what had been promised, since God had planned something better for us so that only together with us would they be made perfect.*' v39-40

The last verse is quite remarkable: '***These were all commended for their faith***'. Both those who received and those who did not receive what had been promised! If God has made promises they will most certainly be fulfilled because it is impossible for God to lie. (Hebrews 6:18) God watches over His Word to see that it is fulfilled. (Jeremiah 1:12) The issue is how and when are they are to be fulfilled.

The reason God gives for them not receiving what had been promised during their earthly lives was that ***God had planned something better!*** Which of us would not be satisfied if God superseded our request with something totally out of this world?

And that seems to be precisely what God has planned. The timing of the fulfilment is in the age to come when they, together with us, are 'made perfect.' The Greek word *'teleioo'[11]* means 'to finish, to complete, to add to what is yet wanting in order to render a thing full.'

The complete fulfilment of all our prayers will happen in the consummation of all things at the end of the age. We will all be fully healed, delivered, provided for and fulfilled in every possible way. God rewards those who earnestly **seek Him,** not just those who seek from Him.

*'As for me, I shall be vindicated and shall **see your face**; when I awake, **I shall be satisfied with seeing your likeness.**'* Psalms 17:15

*'**You will fill me with joy in your presence**, with eternal pleasures at your right hand.'* Psalms 16:11

We are so rooted in this material world of time and sense; God has to continually lift our horizons to incorporate the unseen realm and its dimensions into our thinking and our prayers. Yes, I believe the angels add their incense to these prayers too. And many of the answers that they send back to the earth with fire from the altar in the form of thundering, lightning and earthquakes, will be in the final consummation at the return of Christ to usher in 'the perfect.'

Royal service

The ministry of angels to the Lord is to serve the King of Glory as royal courtiers in the courts of heaven. For example: In the United Kingdom the Queen has royal servants; likewise God as king of all the earth and king of the whole universe, has His royal attendants.

---

11   Strong's G5048

They wait on him listening for every Word, watching for every gesture and every glance.

*'The Lord has established his throne in heaven, and his kingdom rules over all. Praise the Lord, you his **angels**, you **mighty ones** who do his bidding, who obey his word. Praise the Lord, all his heavenly **hosts**, you his **servants** who do his will.'* Psalms 103:19-21

This verse is written by King David who has an understanding of kingship and the various functionaries who are necessary to operate a government. So he has insights into how Yahweh has set up the government of the universe and how the angelic ranks fill the various offices. He uses four words in these verses to describe the various ranks and functions.

The first word is 'angels' *(Heb. 'malak')*. This is the most basic word for angel used throughout Scripture and it means 'messenger'.

Angels are 'sent' (from Greek *'apostolos'*) on mission by God to communicate his message to someone. They are apostles or messengers of the King. They are his deputies and represent Him to those to whom He has sent them. For example, Gabriel was sent to Daniel, to Zechariah, and to Mary to deliver a message from God.

*'He said, "Daniel, you who are highly esteemed, consider carefully the words I am about to speak to you, and stand up, **for I have now been sent to you.**" And when he said this to me, I stood up trembling.'* Daniel 10:11

*'The angel said to him, (Zechariah) "I am Gabriel. I stand in the presence of God, **I have been sent to speak to you** and to tell you this good news.'* Luke 1:19

*'In the sixth month of Elizabeth's pregnancy, **God sent the angel Gabriel** to Nazareth, a town in Galilee, to a virgin pledged to be married to a*

man named Joseph, a descendant of David. The virgin's name was Mary.'
Luke 1:26

Gabriel's position was to stand in the presence of the Lord. He stood listening for the voice of the Lord, ready to fulfil His orders. Each time he was sent on a mission he fulfilled that mission. That is the stance of the courtier angels. They stand in the presence of the Lord and wait for their assignments. When an angel was sent to Daniel, he was opposed by territorial spirits in the Persian region to which he was sent but was helped by the archangel Michael so that he was ultimately successful although delayed by three weeks.

When Gabriel was sent to Zechariah to announce the birth of a son in his old age, Zechariah did not believe. Gabriel had authority to act on God's behalf and strike him dumb for his unbelief. To refuse to believe an angel of God is to refuse to believe God, so it is a serious affair. Likewise when God sent an angel to lead Israel to the Promised Land he warned Israel not to rebel against the angel as we see here...

*'See, **I am sending an angel** ahead of you to guard you along the way and to bring you to the place I have prepared. Pay attention to him and listen to what he says. **Do not rebel against him**; he will not forgive your rebellion, since **my Name is in him.**'* Exodus 23:20-21

He was an angel on a mission from Yahweh with God's authority, acting in union with God. To rebel against him was to rebel against Yahweh and that was a serious offence against God with serious consequences. By contrast, Mary gave the proper response to Gabriel...

'I am the Lord's servant; may it be to me as you have said.' Luke 1:38

Angels functioning as messengers are also God's **servants** (in Hebrew 'sharath' Psalms 103:20) This word refers to someone who serves. According to Strong[12] it comes from a primitive root that means 'to

---

12   Strong H8334

attend to as a 'menial' or 'worshipper', Gabriel was a high-ranking powerful messenger. It would appear that there are other angels who are of lower rank also doing whatever God requires them to do.

The Divine Council

It would appear from various Scriptures, that some angels of high rank are involved in governmental service, as, for example, a cabinet of ministers with various portfolios. The Psalmist refers to the council of the heavenly beings (Heb. *qadoshim,* holy ones).

'The heavens praise your wonders, Lord, your faithfulness too, **in the assembly of the holy ones.** *For who in the skies above can compare with the Lord? Who is like the Lord among* **the heavenly beings?** *In the* **council of the holy ones** *God is greatly feared; he is more awesome than all who surround him.'* Psalm 89:5-6

There is a divine council composed of high-ranking heavenly beings, holy ones, who meet in assembly where God presides. He is more awesome than all who surround him! Yet it seems that he includes these created heavenly beings as part of his divine council.

The prophet Zechariah refers to it as well…

'The angel of the Lord gave this charge to Joshua: "This is what the Lord Almighty says: 'If you will walk in obedience to me and keep my requirements, then you will govern my house and have charge of my courts, and I will give you a place among these standing here.' Zechariah 3:6-7

In this scene we see God sitting in the courts of heaven and satan bringing a charge against Joshua, the high priest. There are angels operating in the courts and participating in the defence of Joshua, taking off his filthy clothes and putting rich garments on him.

Zechariah, the prophet, is also there and participating, saying, '*put a clean turban on his head.*' Zechariah 3:5 But it is the angel of the Lord (Jesus) who offers Joshua a place of governance in God's house and a place in the heavenly council if he walks in obedience to the Lord and keeps his requirements.

Therefore, we see that the heavenly council is a place where high-ranking angels, prophets and high-ranking spiritual leaders are given access. Jeremiah operated from there. In contrast God castigates the false prophets because they have not stood in his council.

'But which of them has stood in the council of the Lord to see or to hear his word? Who has listened and heard his word? But if they had stood in my council, they would have proclaimed my words to my people and would have turned them from their evil ways and from their evil deeds.' Jeremiah 23:18, 22

Jeremiah is not talking here about the gift of prophecy which all believers are encouraged to seek, though not all exercise it. (1 Corinthians 14:1-3) He is talking about someone who is called by God to the office of prophet, whose duty, like that of the angels, is to listen and watch, to hear and see what God is saying or doing and then proclaim God's Word and carry our God's works. This means positioning oneself in God's presence, in God's council from where God governs.

Amos declares:

'Surely the Sovereign Lord does nothing without revealing his plan to his servants the prophets.' Amos 3:7

The Hebrew word translated 'plan' is '*sod*', which means 'counsel, council, assembly.'[13] It is the same word used by Jeremiah to refer to God's council. It is the circle of God's intimates where He gives

---

13   Strong H5475

his counsel to his prophets in the presence of angels. Angels are often involved in the process of communicating God's Word to his prophets, as we see frequently in Daniel and Zechariah and other places.

We can now see that angels are in royal service as God's courtiers, some serving in high ranks in God's council, like cabinet ministers, and others as personal attendants ready to do whatever God wants. They are our fellow servants, in that we too are in royal service, some serving in God's council as apostles or prophets and others as God's attendants ready to do whatever God wants us to do. They are our model of service to God.

Military service

Angels also are engaged in military service in God's heavenly army. This is a very prominent part of their activity. In fact, there are probably special legions of warrior angels for whom this is their primary function. David describes them in Psalm 103:21 as warrior angels or 'hosts' (Heb. *tseba'ah*). It can refer to a host of stars, a host of people or a host of angels. In this case it refers to angel armies. God is frequently called the Lord of Hosts *('Yahweh seba'oth')*. It was the title David used for God when confronting Goliath...

'You come against me with sword and spear and javelin, but I come against you in the name of the Lord Almighty, the **God of the armies of Israel**, *whom you have defied.'* 1 Samuel 17:45

In this case the hosts referred to are the armies of Israel, but it came to be used for the heavenly armies of angels as well. *'Who is this King of glory?* **The Lord of hosts**, *He is the King of glory.'* Psalm 24:10

Psalm 103:20 says, *'Praise the Lord, you His angels, you mighty ones who do his bidding, who obey his word.'*

The Hebrew for 'mighty ones' is *Gibbor* which means powerful, warrior, champion. It is used also in Scripture for men, such as Goliath. Angels are powerful warriors like Goliath. It is also used of the Lord Himself.

'The Lord is a **warrior** *('Gibbor'); the Lord is his name. Pharaoh's chariots and his army he has hurled into the sea.'* Exodus 15:3-4

We need to realise that what is happening in this world is a shadow of what goes on in the heavenlies. As there are wars and battles taking place in the world, there are also wars and battles taking place in the heavenlies. Ask Daniel. Jesus knew about the warrior angels available to him. Matthew 26:53, *'Do you think I cannot call on my Father, and he will at once put at my disposal* **more than twelve legions of angels?'**

A legionnaire in the Roman days was not just any soldier who joined up, but handpicked and chosen to be trained as a warrior for the Roman Empire. Jesus is clearly saying here, that His Father would put at His disposal, (under my command) more than 12 legions,[14] which is at least 62,400 warrior angels!

There are battles to be fought in the heavenly realm and in the earthly realm. God is a warrior and he has multitudes of warrior angels, mighty champions at his command. Jesus himself is their commander-in-chief. That is how he revealed himself in his preincarnate form to Joshua before the battle of Jericho.

'Now when Joshua was near Jericho, he looked up and saw a man standing in front of him with a drawn sword in his hand. Joshua went up to him and asked, "Are you for us or for our enemies?" "Neither", he replied, "but as **commander of the army of the Lord** *I have now come". Then Joshua fell face down to the ground in reverence, and asked him, "What message does my Lord have for his servant?" The commander of the Lord's army replied, "Take off your sandals, for the place where you are standing is holy." And Joshua did so.'* Joshua 5:13-15

---

14 A Roman legion was roughly of brigade size, composed of 4,200 infantry and 300 cavalry in the republican period, extendable to 5,200 infantry.

The Invisible Army

God has an invisible celestial army of warrior angels and a visible terrestrial army of his human followers with their generals; Jesus being the commander of both.

The battle of Jericho that we can read about in Joshua 5, was going to require collaboration between both armies and an unusual military strategy. Joshua needed to know exactly what his part of the siege of Jericho was and to be willing to execute it precisely, and then the unseen army would spring into action and bring the walls down.

The strategy worked perfectly and shows us how important it is for us to know God's strategy in spiritual warfare. And never be put off by not fully understanding the all-knowing Almighty God and His ways. Operate in what He has shown you and ask for a greater understanding; in God there is always more! We do not act alone but are part of a wider picture of working with God and His angels.

On one occasion God directed us to encircle the whole region of Occitanie in prayer. We drove 1750 kilometres, over a four-day period, praying and worshipping continually. When we had finished, one of our prophetic friends in Ireland told us that she had a vision of the region. In the vision she could see the entire region from above and it seemed to have a dark line around it. But as she zoomed in closer, she saw that it was a wall of angels that God had positioned around the region as we had prayed. God had activated his angel army as we obeyed His instructions and did our part. We must do our part to see God move!

Many times we can forget that we are in a spiritual world with an earthly suit on us, and we try and fight spiritual battles using an earthly means. We can never win like this. We can only win spiritual battles through Christ and under the leadership of the Holy Spirit.

At times when David thought his military intelligence could defeat his enemies, he found out the hard way, and they defeated him. But when he enquired of the Lord, the Commander in Chief, he knew exactly how to overcome the enemy.

*'Once more the Philistines came up and spread out in the Valley of Rephaim; so David enquired of the Lord, and he answered, "Do not go straight up, but circle round behind them and attack them in front of the poplar trees. As soon as you hear the **sound of marching** in the tops of the poplar trees, move quickly, because **that will mean the Lord has gone out in front of you** to strike the Philistine army." So David did as the Lord commanded him, and he struck down the Philistines all the way from Gibeon to Gezer.'* 2 Samuel 5:21-25

David learned the importance of working in alignment with heaven's armies, enquiring of the Lord before embarking on his mission. At a particular time, they would hear the sound of the angelic army marching in the tops of the trees, and by this they would know that God had gone out ahead of them to strike down the Philistine army. God gave him the strategy to pursue and the timing of his action, two crucial factors for success.

One time in the Connacht Outreach Project we delayed activities for two years till we got the signal from the Spirit that it was time to resume again. And when we did so it proved to be the most successful mission in that project.

Listen carefully, David still had to fight in that battle and strike down the Philistines. Yet there were other occasions where God did the fighting Himself with His angel armies. Likewise Isaiah the prophet was sent to tell King Hezekiah that God would protect Jerusalem from the approaching army.

*'I will defend this city and save it, for my sake and for the sake of David my servant." That night **the angel of the Lord went out and put to death a hundred and eighty-five thousand** in the Assyrian camp. When the people got up the next morning – there were all the dead bodies!'* 2 Kings 19:34-35

God had personally promised to defend Jerusalem from the Assyrians and in that one night the angel of the Lord slew 185,000 Assyrian troops! Sometimes the angels fight literal physical battles against people, but mostly they fight against the dark spiritual powers that influence people.

On another occasion King Jehoshaphat sought counsel from the Lord when the land was invaded by a vast army. God clearly told him:

*'**You will not have to fight this battle.** Take up your positions; stand firm and **see the deliverance the Lord will give you**, Judah and Jerusalem. Do not be afraid; do not be discouraged. Go out to face them tomorrow, and the Lord will be with you." Jehoshaphat appointed men to sing to the Lord and to praise him for the splendour of his holiness as they went out at the head of the army, saying: "Give thanks to the Lord, for his love endures for ever." As they began to sing and praise, **the Lord set ambushes** against the men of Ammon and Moab and Mount Seir who were invading Judah, and they were defeated.'* 2 Chronicles 20:15-23

Jehoshaphat and his army did not have to fight physically, but they did have to go out, face the enemy and take up their positions.

They then appointed men to go ahead of the army to sing and praise the Lord and the Lord set ambushes against their enemies by turning them on one another so that they wiped each other out.

This is one of the primary strategies God has given to us as priests of God to lift up God's name above all others who raise themselves against the Lord.

Contemporary Spiritual Warfare

Recently in Toulouse, France, an attempt was made to reawaken the Roman gods that used to be worshipped here. A giant Minotaur was constructed, thirteen metres high and weighing forty-seven tonnes,[15] and called the 'Guardian of the Temple.' It was physically very impressive with mechanical and electronic moving parts so that it could walk through the city, and nearly a million people came to see it just after Halloween. They had a sorcerer to animate it so that it did really seem to be alive with eyes that were sinister and smoke bellowing from its nostrils and making roaring sounds. For many it was just a big cultural event, but for the organisers it was an attempt to use sorcery under the guise of the arts in order to introduce pagan gods to influence the city. It was the priests of these same pagan gods who brought about the martyrdom of St. Saturnin, the first Christian bishop of Toulouse, in 250AD. They were angry with him because their oracles would not work when this godly man passed in front of their temple.

As Christians who had been called to this city, we felt guided by the Lord in the spiritual action we were to take to counter these evil influences. We spent a number of days in prayer and fasting in the House of Prayer. We went to key locations in the city where God would guide us. We lifted up the name of the Lord as the only legitimate God worthy of worship in our city. We repented for the sins of those who were worshipping other gods. We did prophetic acts, took communion, and made decrees aligned with Scripture, and left the matter in God's hands.

Afterwards the Lord showed us that because of our prayers the sorcerers had not been able to animate the Minotaur with the particular spirits they wanted to, but had had to settle for lesser spirits. We later sensed that these spirits too had left, when we went to the new 'temple' to call for the presence of the Lord there.

---

15   La Dépêche du Midi: 31 Octobre, 2018. www.ladepeche.fr

On this occasion my wife and another woman were particularly led to pray in this place. Before going my wife felt fearful. But the Lord assigned two angels, in the form of two mighty eagles, one on either side to accompany her. Her fear disappeared. This was a tremendously reassuring presence and they remained with her for quite some time afterwards. These 'eagles' would have been ferocious to any opposing spirit. Usually our strategy when we go into battle is to focus on praising the Lord and then to do what He shows us to do. When we act in obedience to his instructions, He liberates his angel warriors to do what only they can do.

Offensive and Defensive Strategies

In spiritual warfare, as in military warfare, there are seasons of offensive strategy when we move forward to take ground from the enemy, and there are times of defensive strategy when the enemy is launching an all-out assault against us. Paul describes the defensive posture we are to take in Ephesians 6. We are to put on the full armour God has provided so that we can take our stand against the devil's schemes. **When the evil day comes,** we have to dig in our heels and **stand our ground, stand firm** and **stand against** the powers of the dark world and the spiritual forces of evil.

There have been times in our ministry and church life when we have been under such intense and prolonged attack by the enemy that it has been impossible to move forward with new initiatives.

We had to learn to dig in our heels and hold the ground we had. On one occasion I remember the Lord saying to us, 'put your sword in its sheath.' It was not a time for offensive action but defensive stance. In the military, soldiers are not on the front lines continually. They do a tour of duty, then are pulled back to recuperate, before being sent out again.

On the other hand, there is a danger of being so preoccupied with what the enemy is doing that we neglect our mandate to take the battle to him and release the captives whom we are anointed to liberate through the Gospel. In these situations, the best form of defence is attack. We put him under pressure and engage in our 'trampling' ministry. (Psalm 91:13)

There are battles that higher-ranking angelic authorities fight directly against territorial principalities on our behalf; meaning - there are some battles we do not fight. Our role in these circumstances is to take our place in the heavenly realms at the golden altar with prayer and praise. We operate at the level of the third heaven and at ground level and let God and his angels take care of the authorities operating at the level of the second heaven.[16]

We see this in Daniel, where he fasts and prays and Michael the archangel comes to fight against the prince of Persia to bring the victory to the earth realm. (Daniel 10)

One of the keys of spiritual discernment in leadership is to know when to advance and when to stand and secure the ground we have taken. And can I let you know this? We need to know what battles we are to fight and what battles we are not called to fight.

Like Joshua, we are under the leadership of our great Commander-in-Chief and He knows how to lead so that both work in concert. In this sense, the warrior angels are our fellow servants because we too are in God's army and serve the same Master and fight the same foe. We need to 'take our shoes off' and bow before Him for His directions, and please note, I am not referring to natural shoes!

Taking New Territory

In our ministry in the west of Ireland on several occasions we received

---

16 The first heaven is the natural sky or heaven, the second heaven is the invisible realm where satan operates as prince of the power of the air, the third heaven is where God's throne is and where we are seated with him in the heavenly realms.

clear instructions from the Lord to take new initiatives to reach out to the surrounding towns. At one point we began to pray for a small town in County Galway. I began to encircle it in prayer a number of times and we began to pray for it in our church prayer meetings.

We continued praying for that town along the lines God was guiding us to pray. He had put it on our hearts to pray for a 'Lydia' like the Lydia at Philippi, who opened her heart to the message of Paul and then opened her home for Paul. (Acts 16:13-15) Then one night the Spirit told my wife, "Now is the time to go!" We immediately began to make plans and booked the Community Centre to hold a meeting. We printed invitations and distributed them around the homes throughout the town. We put a team together to travel to that town to worship God, share testimony and preach the Gospel.

A number of people showed up for the meeting and as I was bringing the meeting to a conclusion my wife asked the Lord, 'Who is the Lydia whose heart you have prepared?' The Lord pointed her to a particular woman sitting at the back, so she went to speak with her after the meeting. We discovered that she had just moved into the town about two weeks previously and the first post she had had through the door had been our invitation. Her husband had bought a Bible in a jumble sale seven years previously and had been reading it. She invited us to go and meet with him and we discovered that he had come to an understanding of the Gospel through reading the Bible but did not have any Christian fellowship. This family offered us the use of their home to do Bible studies.

God was away ahead of us! We had booked the Community Centre for another meeting the following week, but in the afternoon before the scheduled meeting the caretaker phoned me to say that we could no longer have the meeting room. It was at very short notice and he would not give me a reason for the cancellation. I pressed him on the matter and he said that it was the religious authorities in the town who did not want us and blocked our booking. At that time in rural Ireland virtually the whole of life was controlled by an authoritarian religion that had no time for vibrant Christianity. It was very like Jerusalem in the time of the early church. It was the religious authorities who persecuted the apostles and forbade them to preach.

But God had already opened the door of a home, so we met there instead. The lady invited some of her neighbours to the first meeting; they were from the Travelling Community who had settled in that town. That first night two of them gave their lives to the Lord and we prayed for them to be filled with the Holy Spirit.

That was the beginning of a whole new move of God among the Travelling People of Ireland. We began to have meetings in different homes and in caravans in towns around the region. God began to move in healing miracles among them and a number of them were baptised in their desire to follow the Lord.

Later we were visited by French Travelling pastors who had been stirred to reach the travelling population of Ireland. They showed video clips of thousands of Travellers at large gatherings worshipping God. This was a great encouragement to our group in Ireland who thought they were the only Travellers in the world who had come to know the Lord.

When God directs us, as soldiers in His army, to move out and take territory from the enemy, we will no doubt meet opposition and even persecution inspired by the enemy. But we do not go alone. When God sends us on a mission he also assigns his angelic warriors to go before us to prepare the way and to go with us to give us the land God has for us to take. Likewise, when God sent the children of Israel to take the territory of Canaan from its current inhabitants, he sent an angel ahead to drive them out.

'My angel will go ahead of you and bring you into the land of the Amorites, Hittites, Perizzites, Canaanites, Hivites and Jebusites, and I will wipe them out.' Exodus 23:23

One night when we were returning to Galway City after one of these outreach meetings, my car mysteriously caught fire. It happened just as I stopped to drop off one of my passengers who immediately ran to his house to get some water to douse the flames. I raised the bonnet to give us access to the source of the fire. Just then two men arrived along the footpath. One of them took off his heavy coat, tucked it around the engine and smothered the flames very successfully, then walked off along the footpath.

When I had taken in the situation, I wanted to thank the man who had so unselfishly taken off his coat on a cold winter's night, something it had not occurred to me to do. When I turned to look in the direction the men had gone; there was no sign of them. They just seemed to have vanished! They didn't hang around to see the outcome of their actions or to talk to us. It seemed most unusual.

I have often reflected on that in succeeding years and wondered if, in fact, they were angels sent on assignment. Thank God for His protecting angels.

We can see that there are these three forms of service that angels give to the Lord: the priestly service of worship, praise and prayer; royal service, standing in the heavenly courts to be sent on mission by God; and military service to fight God's battles against the powers of darkness. In the next chapter we will see that they serve us as well!

"Angels are God's servants, but He sends them to serve us."

CHAPTER 4

How do Angels minister to us?

We have seen from Hebrews 1:14 that angels are of God servants. But they serve us as well, though in a different way.

*'Are not all angels ministering spirits **sent to serve** those who will inherit salvation?'*

The Greek word for 'serve' here is different from the word used earlier for serving God or ministering to God, which was *'leitourgos'*. The expression used for serving us is *'eis diakonean'*.

It means to 'help', 'to exercise a ministry towards', to 'serve' us. They are 'sent' to serve us. They are God's envoys to us and they represent Him in serving and helping us. As explained earlier, they are not our servants and we are not their master, so we do not 'send' them or command them in any sense. It is God who sends them to serve us when He deems fit.

There are two main aspects of their service to us: they serve us in our personal lives, and they serve us in our ministry.

Personal Ministry

Angels came and ministered to Jesus personally in the wilderness:
'Then the devil left him, and angels came and attended him'. (Matthew 4:11)

It is the Greek word '*diakoneo*' that is used of this personal service. Jesus had just been through a severe time of testing where He had endured forty days of sustained attack from satan with a host of temptations. He had just been anointed by the Holy Spirit for his ministry, but had been led by the Spirit into the desert for the express purpose of being tested by the devil before his ministry could begin. He had to overcome Satan in his own life before He could effectively have authority over him in the lives of others.

The same is true for us: we only have effective authority over satan for ministry to others to the degree that we have established our authority with him by defeating him in our own lives. For example, a schoolteacher is given authority to exercise discipline and control of his/ her class. But he/she has to establish that authority with the pupils in the early days of his/her teaching or else the pupils will run riot, and he/she will not be able to teach. When I was at school some of our teachers had clearly established their authority and we respected them. Others had not and we boys made their lives a nightmare. Likewise, we have all been given authority over satan (Luke 10:19) but we have to establish that authority in practice, first in our personal lives, then in our ministry.

Jesus had to face satan as a human being filled with the Holy Spirit. While Scripture makes it abundantly clear that Jesus was fully God, it is also clear that in his incarnation he laid aside his divine prerogatives in order to live his life on earth fully as a man. (Philippians 2:5-11) Otherwise his temptations were not real temptations, since God cannot be tempted by evil, and they would hold no inspirational benefit for us. To be a faithful and compassionate high priest to help us in our trials and temptations, He had to face them with the same resources as us, as people filled with the Holy Spirit. He did so, and defeated satan at every turn, having been tested in all points as we are, except that He never sinned.

However, when these tests were over, Jesus, as a man who had been fasting for forty days, was clearly hungry and exhausted. That is when the angels came and served him. We don't know what kind of service they rendered, but they served him in the ways that He needed.

Angels strengthen us when we feel overwhelmed

When Elijah was in a similar situation an angel came and cooked for him!

'All at once an angel touched him and said, 'Get up and eat.' He looked around, and there by his head was some bread baked over hot coals, and a jar of water. He ate and drank and then lay down again. The angel of the Lord came back a second time and touched him and said, 'Get up and eat, for the journey is too much for you.' So he got up and ate and drank. Strengthened by that food, he travelled for forty days and forty nights until he reached Horeb, the mountain of God.' 1 Kings 19:5-8

Elijah had been in a major spiritual battle to save his nation from worshipping foreign gods. He had called a drought on the land as a punishment for their idolatry and also to demonstrate to the people that it was Yahweh who brought the blessings of rain, productivity and fertility, not Baal and Ashtoreth to whom the people had been sacrificing.

He called for a showdown with the 450 prophets of Baal and 400 prophets of Ashtoreth whom Jezebel, the queen, had been sponsoring. He challenged the prophets of Baal to build an altar and put a bull on it as a sacrifice to their god, and he would do likewise. But neither was to put fire to it, but rather call on their god to send the fire. The prophets of Baal accepted the challenge and they agreed:

'The god who answers by fire – he is God!' 1 Kings 18

Elijah had won the showdown as Yahweh sent fire to the prophet's sacrifice, even though he had doused his sacrifice with barrels of water, but there had been no response from Baal.

When all the people saw this, they fell prostrate and cried, 'The Lord – he is God! The Lord – he is God!' 1 Kings 18:39

That, incidentally, was the meaning of Elijah's name – Yahweh is God! It was a great victory for Elijah. He then set himself to pray for rain after three and a half years of drought. Then he prophesied to Ahab the king to get in his chariot and get back to town quickly because heavy rain was on the way. Ahab did so and Elijah ran ahead of Ahab's chariot all the way to Jezreel, a distance of about thirty-four kilometres, (21 miles) a truly supernatural feat!

When Ahab got back to Jezreel he told his wife, Jezebel, all that Elijah had done, and how he had killed all her prophets. Jezebel sent a messenger to Elijah to say,

'May the gods deal with me, be it ever so severely, if by this time tomorrow I do not make your life like that of one of them.' 1 Kings 19:2

She took an oath on her own life to kill Elijah. Ahab the king did not intervene to stop her, even though he had seen incontrovertible evidence that Baal was impotent and Yahweh really was God. Ahab was the legitimate king and through marrying Jezebel, a priestess of the Phoenician gods, he had opened the door to idolatry in the nation. Elijah, as prophet, had carried out his mandate and dealt with the false prophets. It was now up to the king to deal with the queen, the high priestess who had given them legitimacy. Ahab failed to do so and Elijah was extremely disappointed to the point of feeling a failure and fleeing from Jezebel. He sat down under a tree and asked God to take his life.

Elijah had bravely faced the 850 false prophets, but he ran away in fear when Jezebel's oath was pronounced. He was now being confronted by the higher-level demonic power that lay behind the false prophets. On top of that, he was no doubt emotionally and physically exhausted and thus very vulnerable. This all combined to bring him to a place of depression, despair and death wishes.

That's when the angel showed up and touched him. He was tired and hungry and what he needed was very practical – food and sleep. So the angel prepared a meal for him and left him to get some more rest. Then the angel came back and touched him again and said *'Get up and eat, for the journey is too much for you.'* That was some angel food! It strengthened him to such a degree that he was able to travel forty days to Horeb, the mountain of God.

There God would meet with him and give him his next assignment. He was to anoint successors who would finish the job he had started and anoint a king to replace Ahab, a king who would then deal with Jezebel and return the nation to worship God. The first angelic meal and prescribed rest was to help Elijah recover from his exhaustion. The second was to strengthen him for his next assignment. We often need both!

Angelic help became vital to Elijah at his moment of personal weakness. God knew exactly what he needed and sent an angel to supply that need.

A lady recently told me about her grandfather, a Polish man, who had been in prison for his faith in the Communist era. He was extremely tired, cold and hungry. One day a man came into his cell and brought him a bowl of soup and a blanket. Till the end of his life he believed that it was, in fact, an angel. God had seen him in his extremity and had sent an angel to bring practical help. This greatly encouraged him and strengthened him in his remaining time in prison.

As with Jesus and Elijah, angels are assigned to serve us personally in times of great personal need. That is one of their tasks and we can be grateful to God for them, as was this Polish man.

They can be sent to strengthen us when we feel overwhelmed just as Jesus experienced angelic strengthening in Gethsemane.

'Jesus went out as usual to the Mount of Olives, and his disciples followed him. On reaching the place, he said to them, 'Pray that you will not fall into temptation.' He withdrew about a stone's throw beyond them, knelt down and prayed, 'Father, if you are willing, take this cup from me; yet not my will, but yours be done.' **An angel from heaven appeared to him and strengthened him.** *And being in anguish, he prayed more earnestly, and his sweat was like drops of blood falling to the ground.'*
Luke 22:39-44

One of Jesus' greatest tests was that in Gethsemane. He described it as 'the hour of darkness' when all of hell was let loose to unleash its dark powers against Him. He was in intense agony to the extent of sweating blood, a medically unusual occurrence reflecting the intensity of His spiritual anguish.

The Greek word used to describe His anguish, *'agonia'*, refers to a severe mental and emotional struggle producing anguish. He felt abandoned by His Father as the weight of the sin of all humanity came pressing on Him as He faced the cross. The temptation to give up was no doubt very real, as was His commitment to press through to do His Father's will. In the heat of the combat an angel from heaven appeared to Him and strengthened Him. God sent an angel to impart spiritual, emotional and physical strength to Him.

Thank God for his ministering angels who are sent to strengthen us in our struggles! It was in a situation where my wife felt totally overwhelmed by the challenge she felt that an angel came to sit beside her and strengthen her. He said to her, *your weakness is a treasure, because when you are weak, I am detailed to help you.* These words have become etched in her mind and continue to have a strengthening effect as we continue in our assignments together.

Angels sustain us or deliver us when we are in distress

'In all their distress he too was distressed, and the angel of his presence saved them. In his love and mercy he redeemed them; he lifted them up and carried them all the days of old.' Isaiah 63:9

God is affected by the feelings of his people. It is not just Jesus in His humanity who feels with us in our weakness. The Father is not so removed from His creation that He is untouched by people's suffering. This Scripture clearly teaches us that He feels distress when we feel distress. In the context it is referring to the children of Israel who were suffering in slavery in Egypt. In love and mercy He intervened to redeem them; He lifted them up and gently carried them.

In one particular situation, when they were being pursued by the Egyptian army, the angel of the Lord stepped between the terrified Israelites and the Egyptian army and protected them miraculously.

'Then the angel of God, who had been travelling in front of Israel's army, withdrew and went behind them. The pillar of cloud also moved from in front and stood behind them, coming between the armies of Egypt and Israel. Throughout the night the cloud brought darkness to the one side and light to the other; so neither went near the other all night long.' Exodus 14:19-20

The angel of the Lord came to their help; he came to Moses, in a flame of fire in a bush to send him to deliver the children of Israel. Likewise, God sent an angel to Gideon to send him to deliver Israel from the Midianites. That seems to be God's more usual way of operating.

Men and angels are both in his service and he usually enlists both to execute his will. In both situations God acted when he saw the distress of his people.

The Mother of the Arabs

Theologians talk about the law of first mention. The Bible is a book of unfolding revelation through the history of God's dealings with people. The first reference to a particular doctrine usually lays the foundation and subsequent references build on that foundation. Most foundational doctrines are introduced in Genesis, the book of beginnings. For example, creation, the fall of man, the doctrine of sin and justification by faith are all introduced in Genesis, and then explained and illustrated in more detail as Scripture unfolds.

When the Bible makes explicit reference to angelic help for the first time, I believe that is significant. So when an angel appears to help a servant girl who is mistreated and abused by her mistress in her pregnant condition, it reveals something important about the heart of God for women, for the abused, for the under-privileged, for the single pregnant girl and for the Arab people who issued from Hagar's womb.

In Genesis 16, Abraham's wife Sarah had been unable to have any children and was getting well past the age when that could happen naturally. So, in accordance with a custom prevalent at the time in her cultural background, she offered her Egyptian servant Hagar to Abraham hoping to have a child by her. Without consulting God on the matter, Abraham went along with his wife's suggestion thinking that this might be the way God's promise to give him a son would be fulfilled.

When Hagar saw that she was pregnant, she despised her mistress and her inability to have children. Sarah, who was no doubt hurting and smarting from her barrenness, which was considered a curse, reacted to Hagar's taunting with vicious abuse and maltreated her. This must have been quite severe to force Hagar to flee in her pregnant condition, as there were no social security provisions and starvation would be inevitable, Abraham would not be able to continue to provide for her.

This is when an angel came to her near a well in the desert and told her how to proceed.

Firstly, she had to return to her mistress and submit to her. She would have to change her attitude from one of despising her to one of respecting her. God's provision for her at this stage was still to be in the household of Abraham.

The angel of the Lord also said to her: 'You are now pregnant and you will give birth to a son. **You shall name him Ishmael,** *for the Lord has heard of your misery. He will be a wild donkey of a man; his hand will be against everyone and everyone's hand against him, and he will live in hostility towards all his brothers.' She gave this name to the Lord who spoke to her:* **'You are the God who sees me,'** *for she said, 'I have now seen the One who sees me.'* Genesis 16:11-13

Secondly, God named her son Ishmael, which means 'God hears', because God heard her in her distress. Every time she would call her son in the years ahead she would remember that God has heard her in her distress. Furthermore, she gives God the name 'the One who sees me'. Every time she would call on the name of God she would remember that God saw her in her distress.

God sees and hears those who are in distress and it is one of the missions of angels to come to their aid on God's behalf.

My wife, Fran, describes the following situation where God gave her an insight into the angelic realm regarding people who are terminally ill.

"It is difficult to know sometimes how to pray for someone who is terminally ill, and for the loved ones who care for them.

On one such occasion I was shown a large room full of sofas. Behind each sofa stood a beautiful white angel. I was given to understand that each sofa represented a sick one and their carers, who also suffer great stress and fatigue. The angel standing behind the sofa was the celestial helper assigned to them. It was a beautiful place with many colours reflecting on the angels. It made me think of the sanctuary in Psalm 20:2. *'May he send you help from his sanctuary; from Zion may he give you support!'*

In the centre of the room stood Jesus and He wore a simple tunic, dressed, I felt, to serve, rather than in the glorious robes of his kingship. He would look at an angel, and I felt that an assignment had been communicated. The angel left immediately to fulfil his task. In the room there was joy, which stemmed from His total authority for every situation.

I was reminded how qualified Jesus is to be our High Priest. He is our Melchizedek, who understands, supports and empathises with us and who is sending help from the sanctuary. We may feel that all is out of control and that we are being swept along by painful or overwhelming circumstances. But He remains in total control, always!

Even in the midst of the most hopeless situations God is 'the One who sees' and sends angelic help!

Angels are assigned to protect us

The concept of guardian angels is perhaps the most common Christian thinking about angels. Jesus said,

'See that you do not despise one of these little ones. For I tell you that **their angels** in heaven always see the face of my Father in heaven.'
Matthew 18:11

It would appear that an angel is assigned to every child at conception or birth, and there is no biblical record or understanding that the angel's assignment is ever withdrawn or cancelled. The expression 'their angels' would seem to indicate a very personal association of each child with his or her angel. These angels are simultaneously present with the child and also in the presence of God the Father where they behold His face. As mentioned earlier regarding Jacob's ladder, it indicates that angels connect the earth realm with the heaven realm. They can simultaneously be present and active in both realms.

Justin Fontenot of the Prayerful Anglican states that" the guardian angel concept is clearly present in the Old Testament, and its development is well marked. He continues, stating that in the New Testament the concept of guardian angel may be noted with greater precision. Fontenot also cites Jerome, a Church Father, who said: 'how great the dignity of the soul, since each one has from his birth an angel commissioned to guard it.' (Comm. in Matt., xviii, lib. II)." Zanchius says that all the Fathers held this opinion.[17]

There are many historical incidents when people believe that they were miraculously protected by angels. In May and June 1743, Methodists experienced persecution in Wednesbury and Walsall in England and the founder of the Methodist Church, John Wesley, was threatened with death by a mob who dragged him in the rain. However, "Wesley escaped unharmed" and he "believed that he had been protected by his guardian angel."[18]

There was a similar incident early in the ministry of Jesus when the people of His home town tried to throw Him off a cliff, but He miraculously escaped.

---

17   https://en.wikipedia.org/wiki/Guardian_angel
18   John Wigger, (September 2009) American Saint: Francis Asbury and the Methodists. Oxford University Press. p. 25.

'All the people in the synagogue were furious when they heard this. They got up, drove him out of the town, and took him to the brow of the hill on which the town was built, in order to throw him off the cliff. But he walked right through the crowd and went on his way.' Luke 4:28-29

There is no specific mention of an angel in the incident, but angelic intervention seems the most likely explanation. The crowd were clearly furious and, incited by religious fervour, were bent on their evil plan. But somehow, Jesus inexplicably walked right through the crowd and went on His way unharmed. Many of the incidents of supernatural protection that one hears have often got features that can only be explained by supernatural angelic activity. But since the angels usually don't show themselves visibly as angels one has no 'objective evidence' that it is indeed angels who have provided protection.

One of my mother's favourite Bible verses was, *'The angel of the Lord encamps around those who fear him, and he delivers them.' Psalm 34:7* She would particularly quote this when she would go to drive the car, which she did rather infrequently as she was not a very confident or competent driver. I used to think that it was the other road users that needed more protection when she hit the roads! But she never had an accident or suffered any injury.

She would often claim this promise and pray it for our family growing up in the Troubles of Northern Ireland, when many of our peers were shot or killed in the violence which pervaded the so-called Murder Triangle where we lived. None of us were killed or injured in any of the many bomb blasts which occurred daily during that period. Our church building was damaged five times by explosions in the vicinity and eventually a new church had to be built in a different location.

A couple of years ago I met a man in Perpignan in France, who recounted his experience of angelic intervention which saved his life. He fell from a fifth floor balcony and was plunging head first towards the concrete ground below. In mid-fall an angel intervened and turned him around so that he landed on his feet. Although he was badly injured and was several months recovering, including the miraculous healing of some broken bones in his leg, he eventually made a full recovery. Had he hit the ground head first he would have had no chance of survival. He, his wife and young family were extremely grateful to God for angelic intervention which saved his life.

One might well ask why the angel didn't prevent him from falling in the first place, or from getting hurt in the fall. I'm sure that there are many situations of angelic intervention of which we are not even aware. In short, we do not know why they intervene in some situations and not in others, and in some ways and not in others. But we are thankful to God when they intervene. It possibly has to do with how well we are living within the protective walls of faithfulness to God's covenant and actively praying and believing for God's protection.

Angelic Protection

Psalm 46 is a wonderful Psalm declaring God's protection over his people...

'God is our refuge and strength, a very present help in trouble. Therefore, we will not fear, Even though the earth be removed, and though the mountains be carried into the midst of the sea; though its waters roar and be troubled, though the mountains shake with its swelling. Selah

There is a river whose streams shall make glad the city of God, the holy place of the tabernacle of the Most High. God is in the midst of her, she shall not be moved; God shall help her, just at the break of dawn. The nations raged, the kingdoms were moved; He uttered His voice, the earth melted. The Lord of hosts is with us; the God of Jacob is our refuge. Selah

*Come, behold the works of the Lord, Who has made desolations in the earth. **He makes wars cease** to the end of the earth; He breaks the bow and cuts the spear in two; He burns the chariot in the fire. Be still, and know that I am God; I will be exalted among the nations, I will be exalted in the earth! **The Lord of hosts is with us; the God of Jacob is our refuge.***'

It is the Lord of angelic armies who is the refuge for Israel. It is the angelic hosts who guard the people of God. A very poignant example of this is when Elisha was sought by the king of Syria and the Syrian army was sent to arrest Elisha, but the invisible army of God protected the prophet.

'Then he sent horses and chariots and a strong force there. They went by night and surrounded the city. When the servant of the man of God got up and went out early the next morning, an army with horses and chariots had surrounded the city. 'Oh no, my lord! What shall we do?' the servant asked. 'Don't be afraid,' the prophet answered. 'Those who are with us are more than those who are with them.' And Elisha prayed, 'Open his eyes, Lord, so that he may see.' Then the Lord opened the servant's eyes, and he looked and saw the hills full of horses and chariots of fire all round Elisha.' 2 Kings 6:14-17

The king of Syria had sent 'a strong force' (NKJV 'a great army') with horses and chariots to capture Elisha. But the angelic army sent to protect Elisha outnumbered them. Elisha saw this army of fiery horsemen and chariots surrounding him with his spiritual eyes, while his servant did not. Consequently, his servant was full of fear while Elisha had faith to know God was on his side. Scripture does not give any sense that the Syrian army saw this angelic army. But Elisha, then prayed,

'Strike this army with blindness. So he struck them with blindness, as Elisha had asked. Elisha told them, 'This is not the road and this is not

the city. Follow me, and I will lead you to the man you are looking for.'
And he led them to Samaria.' 2 Kings 6:18-19

The knowledge of God's greater army of angels protecting him emboldened Elisha to act in faith and ask God to blind the whole Syrian army. God led them into Samaria where Elisha gave them into the hands of the king of Israel. Then the Lord opened their eyes.

So often God's people are controlled by fear and we do not have the boldness to do the works God has ordained for us to do. The enemy wants us to see its 'great army' of demonic forces that are out to 'get us' if we take spiritual initiatives against him. We fear failure, we fear rejection, and we fear what others may think of us. The fear of man is a snare, a trap of the enemy.

The devil's main weapons against us are his army of fears that paralyse us from taking bold action to advance the kingdom of God. We need to be more consciously aware of God's protective angelic army which is more than adequate to face any foe. We are often more like Elisha's servant than Elisha. We need to pray that our spiritual eyes will be opened to see the true spiritual realities.

As Romans 8:31 states: *'If God is for us, who can be against us?'*

What about Suffering?

The battles we face are not to be minimised, nor are the powers of the enemy who opposes us. But it's very important that we keep things in biblical perspective and have our minds aligned with God's view of things.

'Who shall separate us from the love of Christ? Shall trouble or hardship or persecution or famine or nakedness or danger or sword? As it is written:
'For your sake we face death all day long; we are considered as sheep to

be slaughtered.' No, in all these things we are more than conquerors through him who loved us. For I am convinced that neither death nor life, neither angels nor demons, neither the present nor the future, nor any powers, neither height nor depth, nor anything else in all creation, will be able to separate us from the love of God that is in Christ Jesus our Lord.' Romans 8:35-39

We are sentenced to victory; but wait; that victory may include trouble or hardship or persecution or famine or nakedness or danger or sword! And we must be prepared to go through them as much as be rescued from them. Likewise, Peter was delivered from prison by an angel (Acts 12:6-11), yet James was not. (Acts 12:2)

Throughout history, angelic intervention has miraculously saved the lives of many. But equally many have been martyred for their faith. This is amply illustrated in the history of the Huguenots in France by Pierre Demaude in *Le Réveil des Cevennes,*

What is vital and absolutely guaranteed is that the enemy cannot separate us from the love of God in Christ under any circumstances. Our eternal security in God's love is guaranteed.

When Jesus commissioned his disciples and sent them out with authority to heal and cast out demons, he warned them that they would be persecuted just as he was. They were going into enemy territory to free captives from Satan's power. So, it would be real, ground-level spiritual warfare. It would be all-out war, and in a war there are casualties. But he also told them not to fear those who can kill the body but cannot kill the soul. Rather they were to fear the one who could destroy soul and body in hell! (Matthew 10:28) Our focus should be on our King not on what the enemy can do! A willingness to suffer for the sake of Christ is part and parcel of the Christian mindset.

Peter tells us in 1 Peter 4:1 to arm ourselves with this attitude...

'Therefore, since Christ suffered in his body, **arm yourselves** *also with the same attitude.'*

As we approach the end times, Scripture makes clear that the battle will greatly intensify and that satan is angry, knowing his time is short. This will cause him to wage a more vicious war on the children of God. (Revelation 12:10-17) Even in the intensity of that great tribulation the woman, who represents the people of God, is given the wings of a great eagle so that she may fly away to a safe place.

This symbolises angelic help since one of the faces of the cherubim is the face of an eagle. We need to be clear that God's promises of angelic protection do not necessarily mean that we will not suffer.

Pressing through for Revelation

We once faced a traumatic situation in our family where we suffered intensely in a way that we never expected. It was so overwhelming that it led us to doubt the promises of God regarding protection.

Like many Christians, we had assumed protection was automatic to the child of God. But then someone in our family circle faced psychological, physical and spiritual problems from the age of ten. Things degenerated in adult years leading to the breakdown of his marriage and further emotional, physical and spiritual breakdown which took years to recover from. We could not understand why, given all the promises of God's protection which we ardently believed.

This was quite traumatic for my wife and myself and led to lots of questioning and an undermining of our confidence in God and His Word. I came to the place where I could no longer believe God's promises of protection in Psalm 91. Do you remember how it starts?

'Whoever dwells in the shelter of the Most High will rest in the shadow of the Almighty. I will say of the LORD, HE IS MY REFUGE AND MY FORTRESS, MY GOD, IN WHOM I TRUST.'

It is a serious matter when a preacher of the Word begins to doubt the Word for himself! For me it meant that I had to set my face to meet God at a new level.

You see, suffering often serves that purpose. If our knowledge of God is tenuous or shallow, we may respond to suffering by abandoning God or at least growing cold in our affections for Him. But if our faith in God is deep rooted it can drive us to seek God and encounter Him at a deeper level.

The Bible is not a textbook with neat and tidy answers to every human problem. It is the story of men and women in history who engaged with God in the rough and tumble of life on a fallen planet.

Job was a man who faced calamity in every level of his life. His family was wiped out in a series of disasters. He suffered financial collapse and his health caved in. His wife felt she could no longer support him in his faith and his friends turned on him. He became depressed, despairing and longed for death. He got angry with God and demanded answers but no answers came, especially to the big question, 'Why?'

This is a question that most of us are scared to ask God. But do you know that God is not afraid of our questions? They don't knock Him off His throne!

When Job engaged honestly with God, spilling out his feelings and questions, he eventually began to get glimmerings of insight. Hope began to arise again,

'Though he slay me, yet I will hope in Him.' Job 13:15

He began to get revelation of a heavenly intercessor who was pleading with God on his behalf, and that this advocate was his friend. The truth of this revelation only came into full view in the New Testament where Christ is revealed as our intercessor, advocate, friend and high priest.

'Even now my witness is in heaven; **my advocate** *is on high.* **My intercessor is my friend** *as my eyes pour out tears to God; on behalf of a man he pleads with God as one pleads for a friend.'* Job 16:19-21

Revelation often comes only when we are pressed almost to breaking point; it is often then that we break through to the heavenly realm and receive revelation. Job's story happened even before the Torah was written so he had no Bible for revelation. Be he pressed through with God, finding himself saying things that were arising deep out of his Spirit and could only have come by revelation of the Holy Spirit. One such statement that came from deep within was...

*'***I know** *that my redeemer lives, and that in the end he will stand on the earth. And after my skin has been destroyed, yet in my flesh I will see God; I myself will see him with my own eyes – I, and not another. How my heart yearns within me!'* Job 19:25-27

Where did Job get that profound knowledge from? Only by revelation from the Holy Spirit in a deep encounter with God. A revelation of a Redeemer who would stand on the earth in the last days!

A revelation of a physical resurrection after death, burial and disintegration!

A revelation of a personal meeting with and seeing God Himself! And a heart longing for God! He gains the understanding that God is testing him and that, when he has passed the test, he will come forth as gold. (Job 23:10) Eventually after the process of suffering and questioning, and the understandings he has gained deep in his spirit, God shows up and speaks to Job.

Can I ask, what value do we place on hearing from God? What price are we willing to pay for such a divine encounter?

In the end God does not answer Job's questions. He doesn't have to! God is silent. Job is satisfied with this deeper encounter with God which led to a deeper knowledge of God.

'My ears had heard of you, but now my eyes have seen you!' Job 42:5

There is no substitute for divine encounter in which God imparts a **_knowing_** to our spirits. It is not necessarily a knowing of answers to our questions, but a personal knowing of God and of some certainties that he engraves on our heart that give us a solid place to stand in a world of turmoil and uncertainty. After his encounter with God, Job acknowledges that in his grief and despair he had spoken of things he did not understand, 'things too wonderful for me to know.' Job 42:3

I once heard a preacher say that God teaches us nothing through suffering, that He teaches us everything through His Word. He had the temerity to say that in my church, and my response was to follow it with six weeks of teaching from the book of Job. Let us not also forget the New Testament where Paul taught the young Christians, whom he had just brought to faith in Christ, that it was through many trials and tribulations that they would enter into the kingdom. (Acts 14:22)

It should concern us that there is a school of teaching that focuses on victory, success and prosperity so much that it neglects other important Scriptural truths.

Such unbalanced teaching does not equip people to live in a world where there is lots of suffering. It certainly does not equip people to live in the end times when suffering for our faith will become more prevalent in the Western world, as it already is in many countries.

To return to my own story of questioning God's protection, I determined to meet God on the issue, and while I didn't receive any clear answers from God either as to the question why, I certainly came to a place of renewed trust and confidence in God and His Word. I ended up pinning Psalm 91 in its entirety on the wall of my prayer cabin, highlighting this verse about angelic protection!

'For **he will command his angels concerning you to guard you in all your ways;** *they will lift you up in their hands, so that you will not strike your foot against a stone.'* Psalm 91:11-12

This is a wonderful truth, but we must pay attention to its context which shows to whom it refers.

'Whoever dwells in the shelter of the Most High *will rest in the shadow of the Almighty… If you say, 'The Lord is my refuge,' and* **you make the Most High your dwelling,** *no harm will overtake you, no disaster will come near your tent.'* Psalm 91:1,9-10

It means that we actively choose to live in a place of spiritual safety, dwelling in the presence of the Lord, so close to Him that we are under His wings and covered by His feathers. The picture is of little birds that need to stay close to the mother bird to escape the hunter's trap. Our safety is to live in intimacy with the Lord. From this place of spiritual security, we can be bold and go on the offensive against the enemy knowing God's angelic protection.

When satan quoted Scripture to Jesus to tempt Him to throw Himself off the pinnacle of the temple and make a spectacular display to draw attention and applause, he was trying to lure Jesus with subtlety into a trap by getting Him to leave God's ordained path for Him and get glory for himself. He knew that if he could get Jesus to leave the shelter of His Father's covering and act on His own initiative then the condition attached to this promise would be violated and the promise invalid. Jesus however remained in intimate fellowship with the Father and only did the Father's will.

What follows this verse is also important and shows the victories we can gain over the enemy when we have angelic protection.

'For he will command his angels concerning you to guard you in all your ways; they will lift you up in their hands, so that you will not strike your foot against a stone. **You will tread on the lion and the cobra; you will trample the great lion and the serpent.** *'* Psalm 91:11-13

These are various representations of satan who is described in Scripture as a serpent, when he acts with deception and subtlety, and as a lion who roars to intimidate us with a sense of his power.

When we are dwelling under God's protection, it doesn't mean that we are hiding away from the enemy lest he attack us. On the contrary, we are promised safety when we launch out on the offensive to trample on the works of the enemy. It was in the context of their offensive mission to heal the sick and cast out devils that Jesus said to his apprentice followers:

'I have given you **authority to trample** *on snakes and scorpions and to overcome all the power of the enemy;* **nothing will harm you.** *'* Luke 10:19

Jacob's Angelic Encounters

Jacob had four encounters with angels, each at a significant moment in his life.

In the first one the angels were seen as connecting heaven and earth, bringing the presence of God leading to an encounter with God Himself at Bethel. (Genesis 28:10-22) It was at the time Jacob was fleeing from his brother, Esau, who was threatening to kill him after Jacob had cheated him out of his father's blessing. It was in this encounter that God gave to Jacob the same promises he had already given to Abraham and Isaac about inheriting the land of Canaan, just as he was about to flee the land.

The second angelic encounter came twenty years later when things were getting difficult in Jacob's relationship with Laban, his father in law. This time it was the 'angel of the Lord' who also spoke to him as the God who appeared to him at Bethel. (Genesis 31:11-13)

Most theologians regard the 'angel of the Lord' references to be preincarnate appearances of Jesus Christ, because on one hand He speaks as an angel and on the other hand as God. The purpose of this appearance was to instruct Jacob:

*'Leave this land **at once** and go back to your native land.'*

This was indicating to Jacob that it was God's time for him to enter into his destiny and take his inheritance.

Jacob knew for twenty years what his destiny was and the land he was to inherit, but he didn't know when or how to go about it.

For many of us God speaks to us in our younger years and gives us a sense of destiny. It may be something that we sense deep within our spirits, which is the desire of our hearts and that corresponds to our gifts. Or it may be something that God specifically speaks to us about in a very clear way and puts in our heart. But one of the frustrations for many is regarding the timing of fulfilment. Usually we are not yet ready; God has still a lot of work to do in shaping us and training us for the task ahead. Jacob had to spend twenty years working for a tough boss who cheated him over his wife and changed his wages ten times. We often learn most in the workplace, often in difficult circumstances, under harness to someone else.

Like Elisha who served Elijah, and Timothy who served Paul, we frequently have to serve someone else's vision before the Lord considers it the right time to entrust us with our own.

In determining God's will for our lives there are **three important components - the what, the how and the when; or the vision, the method, and the timing.** Often the most difficult thing to discern is the right timing. In this case the circumstances regarding the relational difficulties with Laban get Jacob thinking and preparing mentally for change. But the determining factor was the angelic encounter which gave him a clear word from the Lord.

I have often found in a time of impending change the Lord begins preparing us mentally. It may be that we begin getting unsettled in our spirit; we sense that change is on the way, but we don't know what or when. This may be combined with difficulties emerging in the current situation or may be provoked by such difficulties. Or it may be just the Holy Spirit communicating the sense of impending change to our spirit to prepare us.

When the time came for us to move from Perpignan I began to sense that an imminent change was on the way but I had no idea what it was. Eric, with whom we were working, began to sense it too and raised the issue. Then I got an invitation to go to Toulouse to teach in the prophetic school 'Melkizédek'. I asked the Lord if we were to accept and he replied, "You've got nothing 'to lose!'" God seems to enjoy a play on words as we see often in the Old Testament prophets.

Jacob's third angelic encounter came shortly afterwards, when he had set out on the journey to return to his native land. Jacob remembered the circumstances in which he had left and was very fearful of his brother. He felt very vulnerable as he made his journey with his wives and young children, flocks and herds and God knew this, so He met him at his point of need through angels.

Jacob also went on his way, and the angels of God met him. When Jacob saw them, he said, 'This is the camp of God!' So he named that place Manhanaim.' Genesis 32:1-2

The word 'Manhanaim' means 'two camps'. With that meaning being understood, there seems to have been quite a contingent of angels in this group. As one would know, a camp is a place of temporary resting while on a journey.

It would seem that when Jacob and his considerable human and animal contingent stopped to camp for the night, that he suddenly became aware that his was not the only camp. There was 'the camp of God', a contingent of angels on a military assignment to camp around Jacob and his camp. They were on protective duty.

Jacob certainly needed divine protection at this crucial juncture when he was about to take possession of his inheritance. Esau had felt that he, as the eldest son, had been robbed of this inheritance by Jacob, and had been nursing his grievance for twenty years. He had failed to access the grace of God to handle his hurts and had gotten very bitter. (Genesis 27:41-42; Hebrews 12:15) The angels had a job on their hands! But they were up to it, so Jacob was preserved and warmly received by his brother.

But Jacob needed one more angelic encounter which changed him dramatically as we read in Genesis 32:24-30.

'So Jacob was left alone, and a man wrestled with him till daybreak. When the man saw that he could not overpower him, he touched the socket of Jacob's hip so that his hip was wrenched as he wrestled with the

man. Then the man said, 'Let me go, for it is daybreak.' But Jacob replied, 'I will not let you go unless you bless me.' The man asked him, 'What is your name?' 'Jacob,' he answered. Then the man said, 'Your name will no longer be Jacob, but Israel, because you have struggled with God and with humans and have overcome.' Jacob said, 'Please tell me your name.' But he replied, 'Why do you ask my name?' Then he blessed him there. So Jacob called the place Peniel, saying, 'It is because I saw God face to face, and yet my life was spared.'

This was an unusual experience: an angel, in human form, wrestling with Jacob. He clearly was more than a man because he had the authority to change Jacob's name to Israel and to declare that he had in fact been wrestling with God. Jacob knew that he had the power to bless him and would not let him go until he did so.

And Jacob was aware that he had in fact seen God face to face in this angelic encounter. The angel touched him in the hip and left Jacob with a limp for the rest of his life, perhaps so that he would never forget this experience.

God comes to us in many ways but his objective is ultimately the same. He wants to bless us, but we have to be persistent and determined not to settle for anything less than the full blessing God has for us. It may mean wrestling with God in prayer through the night hours, perhaps when we are faced with situations that are beyond us.

I began to spend serious time with God in my student years and spent my first whole night of prayer when I was only twenty, then a whole week waiting on God before I graduated. Such times have shaped the course of my life.

When I worked in the Yukon Territory in Northern Canada, it didn't get dark at night in the short summer. I used to walk in the great outdoors with the Lord and at times wrestled with Him in prayer over His call on my life. Even though I never saw angels, God's presence was so real at times that He changed the direction of my life from being an engineer to being a preacher of the Gospel. Jacob was transformed from being a deceiver to being a prince with God.

Life has many ups and downs, challenging difficulties, tests and trials, even unanswered prayers. But we have a choice to make in such situations. Do we run away from God because of our suffering and unanswered questions? Or do we run to God for a deeper encounter and greater revelation of His person? How we respond to such situations is crucial and can be life-transforming. God is not our servant to resolve our dilemmas, but He is our Lord and God to be worshipped and served in all situations, good or bad.

"When God assigns us a task, He also assigns angels to work with us in the accomplishment of that task."

CHAPTER 5

How do Angels help us in ministry?

This is a crucial area for us to understand. For many years, like most Christians I was totally unaware of this aspect of angelic ministry. I was conscious of being dependent on the help of the Holy Spirit and of dependence on His empowering and anointing for ministry, but I had no idea the degree to which this could be administered by His servants the angels. I had become increasingly aware that the gifts of the Spirit were 'God's tools to get the job done,' but my experience of them was rather limited.

In particular, my understanding of the gift of discernment of spirits was limited to the discernment of evil spirits. My wife had functioned effectively in this gift for many years and I had done so to a lesser degree. Functioning together as a team, we had seen God deliver many people from demonic bondage and come into wonderful freedom.

But, to some extent, we had overlooked the fact that there are at least twice as many angels as demons, and that we needed to be aware of their activity in helping us to do what God had called us to do, and not just of the enemy's activity in opposing us. Like many, through ignorance we had not developed this gift of the Holy Spirit. Consequently, we had not obeyed the biblical injunction to 'eagerly desire' this aspect of the gift of discernment of spirits. Derek Prince points out that discerning the presence and activity of angels is an important aspect of the gift of discerning of spirits and that this is crucial for any ministry to operate in the realm of the Spirit.[19]

---

19   The Gifts of the Spirit, Derek Prince: Whitaker House, 2007. p 92

Hebrews 1:14 tells us that the angels are ministering spirits sent to serve or to help the heirs of salvation. We have seen, both in the Scriptures and in personal experience, that angels are sent to serve us in our personal needs, whether for strengthening us in our weakness, delivering us when in distress, or protecting us when in danger. But the Bible is also full of examples of how angels are there to serve and help God's people in their ministry.

Angels are 'sent' or 'apostled' in the same way we are 'sent' or 'apostled' by God to fulfil a particular task or mission. They are sent alongside us to help us and serve us. In other words, when God assigns us a task he also assigns angels to work specifically with us in the accomplishment of that task. When God sends us on a mission, He sends at least one angel, but often more than one, to serve us in that mission. We are sent to serve God and they are sent to serve God alongside us.

The first time I became specifically aware of this was when God sent us on a two-week mission to France a few years ago. As we were putting on our seat belts in the plane at Dublin airport I suddenly became aware that there were three angels on each wing travelling on assignment with us. I didn't see them with my natural eyes but I 'sensed' the spiritual reality of their presence. It was impressed on my spirit in the way the God knows how to impress something on our spirit. I discerned their presence. It launched me into a new consciousness of the reality of being co-sent with the angels on mission.

One of the things that I was struggling with at that time was fluency in my French. It had been over 40 years since I had learned French and I had forgotten a lot and lost fluency. But one of my friends said to me on arrival 'The angels know how to speak French too!' On that trip when preaching in one church I had unusual fluency and freedom in speaking the language, even speaking for forty–five minutes without notes! I don't usually do that, even in English!

Angels, our fellow servants

The apostle John, who was very familiar with the ministry of angels, describes them twice as our fellow servants. In fact it was the angel himself who described his role to John in this way.

'I am a fellow servant with you and with your brothers and sisters who hold to the testimony of Jesus.' Revelation 19:10

The angel seemed to have a better understanding of the nature of his role and function than John did, initially! John was even going to worship the angel, he was so overawed by his presence, but the angel intervened to stop him. In fact, John had to be told a second time not to worship the angel who this time described his role more fully:

'I, John, am the one who heard and saw these things. And when I had heard and seen them, I fell down to worship at the feet of the angel who had been showing them to me. But he said to me, 'Don't do that! **I am a fellow servant with you and with your fellow prophets and with all who keep the words of this scroll.** *Worship God!'* Revelation 22:8-9

This was in the last chapter of Revelation. In 21 of the 22 chapters John writes about the angels and their activities in the heavenly realms, both currently and in the last days. But this seems to be the final revelation that he had as to the exact nature of their role as fellow servants of all God's children who hold the testimony of Jesus. And John had to be told twice for it to sink in! Little wonder, then, that so many of us have never grasped this truth. And yet it seems to be something the Holy Spirit is bringing to the light in these last days.

For many generations after the first century the baptism and gifts of the Holy Spirit that were experienced in the Early Church were little known. But in this past century God has been pouring out his Spirit across the nations and denominations and bringing people into a renewed functioning in ways that were common in the early church. The same has happened with a renewed understanding of the prophetic and apostolic ministries in this past generation. And now it seems that the ministry of angels is yet again being brought more clearly into the open. God is restoring to the end-times church the truths and experiences that were lost in the institutional church, in particular from the fourth century on.

In Scripture there are far more references to angels than there are to the gift of tongues, the gift of interpretation or the gift of prophecy. Yet these have become fundamental to so many since the growth of the Pentecostal and charismatic movements. I expect that the ministry of angels will also come much more into the light as the Holy Spirit pours light on the Scriptures that speak about their ministry. Already in many countries in Africa and Asia, where the culture is more aware of the spirit realm, there is much more experience of angelic ministry. But the Western world has been so conditioned by rationalism and this has so infiltrated the Church that we are slower to acknowledge the reality and ministry of angels. So let us have a conscious awareness of the biblical truth that angels are **our fellow servants.** They serve God alongside us. They understand their ministry that way, and we need to understand it that way as well. We need to have a much more conscious and deliberate approach in our ministry that gives due place to this spiritual reality, rather than considering it as something fringy and extreme, or way-out and somehow suspect.

The Greek word used for 'fellow-servant' in the references above, is 'sundoulous'. Thayer defines this word as meaning: 'a fellow servant, who serves the same master with another; a colleague of one who is Christ's servant in publishing the Gospel; one who with others is subject to the same divine authority in the Messianic economy; of angels as fellow servants of Christians.'[20] Paul uses the same word to refer to Tychicus whom he was sending to encourage the Colossian church.

---

20   Strong G4889

*'Tychicus will tell you all the news about me. He is a dear brother, a faithful minister and **fellow servant (sundoulous)** in the Lord. I am sending him to you for the express purpose that you may know about our circumstances and that he may encourage your hearts.' Colossians 4:7-8*

Jesus, Paul, and other disciples often had a team of fellow servants who travelled with them and served with them in ministry. It is interesting to note that that the angels who travel with us and serve with us in our ministry seem to see their role in the same light. They are an integral part of our ministry team! If only we saw how important they are we might be more effective. **Let us pray, '*Lord, open our eyes*',** as Elisha prayed for his servant.

What a difference between Elisha's faith and consequent actions, and those of his servant who was unaware of the spirit realm and the angelic armies! We are often more aware of the forces against us opposing us. We need to know that there are more with us than against us. This transforms our capacity to speak and act in faith.

Moses faced enormous challenges and opposition in his ministry, both from the demonic forces in Egypt opposing his mission to bring the Israelites out of bondage, and from the grumbling people of God themselves who refused to believe and enter the Promised Land.

'By faith he left Egypt, not fearing the king's anger; he persevered because he saw him who is invisible.' Hebrews 11:27

It was his ability to see in the invisible realm that galvanised his faith and enabled him to persevere against all the odds and become one of the greatest heroes of faith. He had seen the commissioning angel in the burning bush and held on to the vision and mandate.

On one occasion when the people had no water they started to grumble to Moses and even talked about stoning him. Moses cried out to the Lord, *'What am I to do with these people? They are almost ready to stone me.'*

'The Lord answered Moses, 'Go out in front of the people. Take with you some of the elders of Israel and take in your hand the staff with which you struck the Nile, and go. **I will stand there before you** *by the rock at Horeb. Strike the rock, and water will come out of it for the people to drink.' So Moses did this in the sight of the elders of Israel.'* Exodus 17:5-6

By faith Moses saw the invisible God, probably the angel of the Lord, standing in front of him ready to work a miracle of providing water for several million people and their animals, as Moses obeyed God and struck the rock.

The Ministry of Angels is important in Kingdom Ministry

After Jesus' baptism and filling with the Spirit, there are two further spiritual events before Jesus launches into ministry. Both are engagements with the unseen spirit realm, one with the devil and the other with angels. Matthew and Luke both mention his encounter with satan and give more detail about the specific exchanges between the two. Luke does not record the encounter with angels and Matthew just says: *'angels came and ministered to him.'* Matthew 4:11 NKJB We are not given any details about this personal service rendered to Jesus by the angels. The New English Translation renders it: *'angels came and began ministering to his needs.'* The New Living Translation says: *'angels came and took care of Jesus.'* One is reminded of the similar situation when the angels came and ministered to Elijah when he was exhausted after his battle with the powers of darkness in Israel. On two occasions the angel touched him and spoke to him and prepared food for him. It would not be surprising if the angels who ministered to Jesus took care of him in similar ways since he was hungry and no doubt tired and in need of strengthening.

The entire ministry of Jesus was going to involve confrontation with
the unseen realm of spiritual darkness. The spirit realm is the sphere
in which ministry takes place. It touches the human and earthly realm
but it is essentially an engagement in the world of spiritual reality,
where spiritual kingdoms clash with each other. Jesus challenged
people to change their way of thinking because the kingdom of
heaven is at hand, within our reach. With our Western material and
rational mindset we need constantly to refocus our mind to perceive
the parallel world of spiritual realities. The demons and satan, the
angels and Holy Spirit are an integral part of this unseen spirit realm
where ministry takes place. And we see this when Jesus, as a man in
the Judean desert, was plunged right into the full reality of this as part
of his preparation for ministry.

The visible world was formed by activity in the invisible realm – by
the Word of God and the Spirit of God. God spoke the creative Word
and the Spirit incubated that Word, bringing forth the material world.

The spirit realm, therefore, is prior and has priority. In the law of
cause and effect, the cause is in the spirit realm and the effect is in the
natural realm, both negatively and positively. This is true in creation
and in providence. Jesus sustains the physical universe by His powerful
Word. (Hebrews 1:3) It was true in the incarnation and resurrection
of Jesus. It was the Holy Spirit who brought Jesus to conception in
Mary's womb and the Holy Spirit who raised him from the dead. It is
true in healing and, most fundamentally, in salvation.

Salvation is an event that transpires in the spirit realm, in the
human spirit through repentance and faith on the part of man, and
accompanied by spiritual regeneration on the part of the Holy Spirit.
Such a spiritual conversion produces visible effects in the natural
realm as was evident in the conversion of Saul of Tarsus, transformed
from a fire-breathing murderer of Christians to a fiery promoter of
the Christian faith.

The atoning work of Christ on the cross was the most profound spiritual activity in the history of humanity. Jesus, as God's anointed High Priest, offered up to God the sacrifice of His sinless body and His shed blood to atone for the sins of fallen humanity as an act of unparalleled love. By His death and resurrection, He defeated satan and took the keys of death and hell to free from condemnation all who put their trust in Him as Saviour.

The preaching of this Gospel is the powerful, life-transforming, spiritual activity through which God has ordained to save those who believe. The message of the cross is folly to philosophically-minded, Greek thinkers, but it is the power of God unleashed to transform humanity and release them from satan's control. The invasion of this spiritual truth into the deceived and spiritually-blinded minds of unbelievers brings light and salvation. It releases the power of the cross to deliver people from demonic bondages and bring them into the freedom that is in Christ.

Jesus was just about to launch into His earthly ministry, this spiritual activity of proclaiming the Good News of eternal life, the healing of sickness and the deliverance of people from demonic powers. And then He was going to crown His earthly ministry with the culminating cataclysmic event of human redemption on the cross.

Satan was opposing Jesus all the way and was trying to launch a pre-emptive strike to try to subvert Him and lure Him into the illegitimate use of His power for personal ends. But the whole angelic realm, twice as numerous as the demonic, was going to serve, minister, strengthen and protect Him in the midst of diabolic onslaught.

The angels had come in force, summoned by God to worship him at His birth. They were totally committed to His cause right from the outset and all the way through to Gethsemane. They had a crucial role in sustaining Him in His trials, in preparing Him for ministry, and in collaborating with Him throughout.

If that was the case for Jesus, how much more so for us! We have the same enemy and have the same supporting angelic ministry team. We can see how He handles satan as a model and example for us in dealing with any temptation and trial.

Unfortunately, many Christians have arbitrarily chosen to focus on satanic opposition and to ignore angelic support. Consequently, many are inadequately prepared for ministry in the spirit realm. A pre-emptive master stroke of satan!

What then should be our expectations of the angels?

How should we tune in to their presence and ministry and receive what God has sent them to bring?

An important question for us to ask is, how do angels come to us?

They normally come invisibly rather than visibly, although Gabriel appeared visibly to Mary. But then also can come in dreams as they did to Joseph on three occasions.

As spirit beings angels communicate a message to our human spirit, an encouragement, a strengthening or a direction.

For example; an idea that we hadn't consciously thought up, arrives in our mind from our spirit with the accompanying sense of God's presence. Our spirit feels uplifted, a rise in our spirit, a resonance that witnesses to this being of God. Usually we have a heightened sense of God's presence when they arrive.

The gifts of the Holy Spirit are part of God's equipment for ministry. These gifts like 'words of wisdom' or 'words of knowledge' are dropped in our spirit as we tune in to the Holy Spirit. They are pieces of God's knowledge or wisdom that we don't have access to naturally.

In some translations these 'words' are referred to as 'a message of knowledge' or 'a message of wisdom'. As shared earlier, messages are usually carried by messengers and we now are aware that angels are God's messengers. That is their most fundamental function. They are spirit beings and operate under the oversight and instruction of the Holy Spirit who is the executive arm of the Godhead functioning in the earth realm.

God the Father is on the throne of the universe in heaven. He is the Fount and Source of all wisdom and knowledge and rules over all. Jesus, God the Son, is now at the Father's right hand having returned to heaven after His assignment on earth. The Holy Spirit was sent to earth after the resurrection of Jesus to continue His work as that executive arm of the Godhead responsible for God's operations on earth. The angels are His host of messengers administering His multitudinous tasks on earth.

In the Old Testament, the 'angel of the Lord' passages are usually considered to be pre-incarnate manifestations of Jesus.

When the 'angel of the Lord' appears to Joshua it is as commander in chief of God's armies. When Jesus returns to earth He returns as commander in chief of His angelic armies. But in the Acts of the Apostles, and therefore in the Church age, the ministry of angels seems to be linked to the ministry of the Holy Spirit, since it is the Holy Spirit who is currently carrying on the work of God on earth.

Like Jesus, it is important for us to be filled with the Holy Spirit and not only that, but to keep being filled with the Holy Spirit. It is then that we are equipped to deal with the devil and tune in to the ministry of the angels God sends to minister to us and with us.

After Jesus had defeated satan and received angelic ministry He *'returned to Galilee in the power of the Spirit.'* Luke 4:14. He went into the synagogue in Nazareth and announced His ministry. The people who heard Him were amazed at the gracious words He spoke, but they reacted angrily to Him and drove Him out of town. Those religious spirits were so stirred up, obviously inspired by satan, that they took Him up to the top of a cliff to throw Him off to his death. But amazingly He just walked through the midst of them and went His way. An invisible company of angels was evidently on duty as His time for death had not yet come.

When Jesus was dealing with demonically-incited opposition He operated with angelic protection. His ministry was an incursion into the dark spirit realm and was accompanied by angelic ministry through the power of the Holy Spirit.

After Jesus called Nathaniel to be His disciple, He turned to the little group He had so far recruited and said to them:

'Very truly I tell you, you will see heaven open, and the angels of God ascending and descending on the Son of Man.' John 1:51

This was an obvious reference to the ladder Jacob saw in his dream with angels ascending and descending and God at the top. Perhaps Nathaniel had just been meditating on that passage when Jesus, in the Spirit, saw him under the fig tree. It was a picture of heaven and earth connected by the angels.

Jesus was now the ladder connecting heaven and earth, bringing the life of heaven to earth in His person and bringing the Father's Word. The angelic realm from which Jesus had come was now to be operative in the earth as well, through Him and His ministry. This young band of disciples who had just responded to His call could expect to see heaven open and the kingdom of heaven touching earth. The spirit realm would be opened up to their understanding and experience. Angels are an important part of bringing heaven to earth and are integral to kingdom ministry.

We need the same today if we are to be properly prepared for ministry. Angels are integral to the domain of the kingdom of God which we are called to proclaim and demonstrate.

CHAPTER 6

Practical examples of Angelic ministry

Angels transmit commissions to us from God

The angel of the Lord appeared to Moses in flames of fire from within a bush at Mount Horeb. Exodus 3:2 makes it clear that it was God Himself who subsequently spoke to Moses from the bush and commissioned him to go to Egypt to deliver His people. But God appeared to Moses as an angel in the form of a flame that didn't burn the bush. It was a spiritual flame rather than a natural one.

Likewise, Isaiah was commissioned by a vision of the Lord and the seraphim that he saw in the temple (Isaiah 6:1-13). The seraphim are high-ranking glorious angels with six wings, associated with the throne and glory of God.

One of the seraphim took a burning coal from the altar and touched Isaiah's mouth to cleanse and purify him for the prophetic ministry God was sending him to fulfil.

In Revelation 10 John saw an angel coming down from heaven with a little scroll in his hand. Then a voice from heaven said to him: *"'Go, take the scroll that lies open in the hand of the angel who is standing on the sea and on the land.' So I went to the angel and asked him to give me the little scroll. He said to me, "Take it and eat it. It will turn your stomach sour, but in your mouth it will be as sweet as honey." I took the little scroll from the angel's hand and ate it. It tasted as sweet as honey in my mouth, but when I had eaten it, my stomach turned sour. Then I was told, "You must prophesy again about many peoples, nations, languages and kings."* Revelation 10:8-11

In this case John was actually caught up to heaven in spirit and received a commission to prophesy again about many peoples, nations, languages and kings. This commission came to him via an angel who gave him a scroll to eat. The scroll was sweet as honey in his mouth but turned his stomach sour. This illustrates the fact that **when God gives us a commission, we have to consume it so that it becomes part of us.**

Ministry from God is not a little add-on extra in life. It must become an integral part of who we are. There are dimensions to ministry that are gloriously sweet and enjoyable and others that are gut-wrenching and challenging to everything within us. When God calls us as His servants we are indentured to Him for the duration. We are his bond-slaves who, at times, pass through the wine press of our Gethsemane. When the darkness presses in on us we may feel that we can't continue without the angelic strengthening that enables us to say, *'not my will, but yours be done!'* Unfortunately, many do give up and resign their commission. At one particularly dark and trying season I came very close to it. But in the depths of depression and despair God's grace triumphed.

More recently I received a new dimension to my commission. I had been in France for just over two years and had just finished the three-month Melkisedek prophetic school in Toulouse. On the penultimate night we had a celebration and commissioning for the graduating students, where they received their scrolls and were prayed for and prophesied over. The students prepared little prophetic gifts and words for the staff as well. The gift I received was a pair of socks with the words, 'to walk through the nations.'

The following morning, in our final worship time together, I was really caught up in a wonderful way into the presence of the Lord. I received a very strong, almost tangible anointing, which I have come to associate with a strong angelic presence. As I was soaking in this powerful, overwhelming sense of God, I became aware of a scroll being handed down to me from the hand of an angel. As I took it and began to unroll it I saw the words 'To the nations!'

I felt that I had been commissioned from heaven and given an additional mandate to travel to the nations.

Since that time, I have travelled to different nations including Switzerland, South Korea, Japan, Singapore, Israel and Egypt as God began to open up my heart in a new way to intercede for the nations.

Remember, angels are involved in transmitting commissions to us and they accompany us to help us to carry out those commissions.

Angels deliver messages to us from God

When Joseph found out that his fiancée Mary was pregnant, and he knew that he was not responsible, he was in a quandary. Naturally speaking, there could be only one possible conclusion, that she had been unfaithful.

Only one possible course of action was open to him according to the law – to divorce her. He could expose her to open shame and stoning or divorce her quietly. He was considering the latter course of action when God sent an angel to him in a dream with a crucial message to him from God:

'Joseph son of David, do not be afraid to take Mary home as your wife, because what is conceived in her is from the Holy Spirit. She will give birth to a son, and you are to give him the name Jesus, because he will save his people from their sins.' Matthew 1:20-21

That was a crucial message for Joseph, and the timing was critical. It was God's destiny for him that he be the legal father to Jesus and earthly provider and protector for Him and His mother. As a direct descendant of King David and heir to His throne, He would bestow on Jesus the legal right to the throne of David and to be the King of the Jews. He would thus fulfil all the biblical prophecies about the Messiah being the Son of David.

As the 'betrothed' of Mary, he was already married to her by covenant although the covenant had not yet been ratified by sexual union. She was therefore already described as his wife and thus he offered to Mary the protection and provision which she so desperately needed as a young girl in an otherwise vulnerable situation. So Jesus was born of a virgin in a miraculous way so that He could fully claim to come from God and incarnate deity, and at the same time not inherit fallen sinful nature.

On two further occasions an angel appeared to Joseph and delivered strategic messages to Joseph in his father-role of providing protection for the infant Jesus.

First, he was instructed to take the Child and His mother and to flee to Egypt because the cruel Herod wanted to kill Him as a perceived threat to his throne. (Matthew 2:13)

Secondly, he was instructed by an angel in a dream to take the Child and His mother and return to Israel. (Matthew 2:19-20)

God, as the heavenly Father of Jesus, was securing His protection by sending angels to deliver messages to the earthly father to whom He had entrusted the care and upbringing of His Son.

How important it is for parents to realise that their children are entrusted to them by God the Father of all mankind, that He takes

His responsibilities seriously, and that He has angels at His behest to give instructions to the earthly parents concerning the care of their children. For those of us who have children, no matter what age they are, we need to start expecting such angelic messages to be sent to us and be alert to perceive them.

Samson's birth was announced by a message from an angel to his mother who had been barren up till then. She wasn't quite sure if he was an angel so she described him to her husband, Manoah, *'a man of God who looked like an angel, very awesome.'* (Judges 13:6) When she told her husband the message about the special upbringing their child would require, Manoah prayed to God:

"Pardon your servant, Lord. I beg you to let the man of God you sent to us come again to teach us how to bring up the boy who is to be born.' God heard Manoah, and the angel of God came again.' Judges 13:8-9

Manoah enquired of the angel how they were to bring up the child and the angel repeated the instructions he had already given to his wife. When Manoah wanted to prepare some food for the angel, still not realizing it was an angel, the angel told him to offer it as a sacrifice to the Lord. Then something unusual happened:

'And the Lord did an amazing thing while Manoah and his wife watched: as the flame blazed up from the altar towards heaven, the angel of the Lord ascended in the flame.' Judges 13:19-20

In this case, the angel initiated the conversation with the woman. She listened without responding, but her husband interacted with the angel asking for clarification regarding the child's upbringing. He didn't pray to the angel; he prayed to the Lord, but he talked to the angel. It is very clear from Scripture that we are not to worship angels or pray to angels, but we can ask God to send them to us. When they initiate a conversation with us we can speak with them as did Manoah, Daniel, Zechariah and Mary etc.

When God sent an angel to communicate a message to my wife, initially she was unsure if it was right for her to talk to the angel. But eventually we saw from these biblical examples that it is proper to do so. Since then, she has felt free to converse with an angel.

Angels are essentially messengers, and their message may evoke or require a response on our part.

Angels give us assignments and messages to proclaim

Some of the assignments given to us by angels include the specific messages we are to proclaim. For example, Ahaziah, the king of Israel, had fallen from an upstairs window and injured himself. Anxious to know whether or not he would recover, he sent messengers to consult Baal-Zebub, the god of Ekron, rather than consulting the Lord God of Israel. So God sent an angel to Elijah to intercept the king's messengers and give them a message from God to the king.

'But the angel of the Lord said to Elijah the Tishbite, 'Go up and meet the messengers of the king of Samaria and ask them, "Is it because there is no God in Israel that you are going off to consult Baal-Zebub, the god of Ekron?" Therefore this is what the Lord says: "You will not leave the bed you are lying on. You will certainly die!"' So Elijah went.' 2 Kings 1:3-4

Elijah was putting his life on the line, but he was faithful to his assignment and duly delivered the message. And the king died according to the Word of the Lord that Elijah had spoken.

When God gave us an assignment in Occitanie to go through the length and breadth of the land to worship and pray and declare, *"This land belongs to the Lord! Jesus is Lord of Occitanie! Jesus shed his blood for Occitanie! God loves the people of Occitanie!"*

we started off from Toulouse, the capital of the region, and drove South West along the A 64 towards Lourdes lifting up the name of the Lord over the region. Then suddenly a cluster of angels drew alongside and hovered over the car as we drove. Two of them sounded trumpets announcing the message, *Prepare the way of the Lord!*

I had never experienced anything like that before, and the hairs began to stand on the back of my neck. An overwhelming anointing of the Spirit came upon us to proclaim the message the angels had just trumpeted. We continued to sound forth that message and declare it over that area in collaboration with the angels. In this case the angels gave us the message to proclaim and the nature of our assignment in Occitanie.

Angels bring revelation about the unseen spirit realm

The primary example of this is the Book of Revelation, but Daniel and Zechariah also had revealing angels to explain what they were seeing in the spirit realm. The Book of Revelation is introduced as:

'The revelation from Jesus Christ, which God gave him to show his servants what must soon take place. He made it known by sending his angel to his servant John.' Revelation 1:1

The content of the Revelation concerns *'what is now and what will take place later.'* Revelation 1:19

John was invited to come up through a door into the heavenly realm to see what was going on in that realm at the current time and what would unfold on earth in the future, but was already a reality in the realm of *Him Who was and Who is and Who is to come.* God sent an angel to John to impart this revelation to him. The centrepiece of that realm is the throne of God with the Lamb at the right hand of the Father. It is the seat of government of the universe. There is continual worship of the Sovereign Lord of the universe. No matter what was happening on the earth at that time of testing, trial and tribulation for the Church, God was totally in control and was working out His eternal plan.

The angels are active in twenty-one of the twenty-two chapters, carrying out their assignments in heaven and on earth. One of them in particular was interacting with John and giving him insight and understanding of what was going on and what would happen in the future. For example, in chapter 17,

'One of the seven angels who had the seven bowls came and said to me, 'Come, I will show you the punishment of the great prostitute, who sits by many waters.' Revelation 17:1 Then the angel carried him away in the Spirit and showed him a vision of a woman sitting on a scarlet beast with seven heads and ten horns. The angel proceeded to explain what the vision meant.

In the final two chapters, one of the angels came to John and said to him: *'Come, I will show you the bride, the wife of the Lamb.' And he carried me away in the Spirit to a mountain great and high, and showed me the Holy City, Jerusalem, coming down out of heaven from God.'* Revelation 21:9-10

He then proceeded to show him the most wonderful revelation of the New Jerusalem when heaven comes to earth in its fullness. Paradise is restored and the throne of God and the Lamb are the centre of God's eternal kingdom in its culmination.

Then the angel says to John: *'These words are trustworthy and true. The Lord, the God who inspires the prophets, sent his angel to show his servants the things that must soon take place.'* Revelation 22:6

The angel explains that his role is to show God's servants, the prophets, the things that are soon to take place. The angel's role with the prophets Daniel and Zechariah was essentially the same. God gave them visions or dreams and the angels guided them in understanding the meaning of the revelation. This was the case for these particular biblical prophets and I believe it is also the role of the angels for contemporary prophets today.

Not all prophets function in the same way. Some receive their message by 'hearing the Word of the Lord,' some by sensing 'the burden of the Lord,' and others by seeing visions or dreams which require interpretation. This is one of the roles of angels. Those who are 'seers' can therefore expect angelic guidance in interpreting what they see.[21]

The book of Revelation shows that the angels are particularly active in the end times as things accelerate towards the culmination. So we can expect to be increasingly aware of their activity as the warfare intensifies. We need their revelation and guidance to interpret the visions and dreams which are becoming increasingly widespread in the church.

Angels bring the sense of the presence of God

There are times in corporate worship when it just seems that we enter a new dimension of the presence of God. I have experienced these many times. It seems that God is somehow closer and more real, almost tangible. At times lively worship can be transformed into an awesome silence in the presence of God. At these times we can feel that we are standing on holy ground, like the song says:

> We are standing on holy ground,
> And I know that there are angels all around.
> Let us praise Jesus now.
> We are standing in His presence on holy ground.
> (Geron Davis 1983 Meadowgreen Music company)

Often in these times the reality is that angels have shown up and brought the atmosphere of heaven with them. We may or may not see

---

21   For more explanation of the contemporary role of seers see: The Seer by James Goll

them but they have come to bring a deeper sense of God's presence and to help us enter further into the awesomeness of God which they inhabit continually.

When this happens, it is a time to put aside our programmes and linger in God's presence and let God take over the lead. I remember the Spirit saying to me on one occasion, '*Pay attention to what the angels are doing!*' That usually is a clue to what God intends to do at that time. We follow what we see in the Spirit.

Much of our ministry in this season is in intercession, particularly for Occitanie. When we see the angels in action, that guides us in how we are to pray and what we are to do. Sometimes we just contemplate the Lord in his glory when his presence is real like that.

On one occasion when I was in the heavenly places in the awesome presence of God, I sensed that an angel came to speak to me. What he impressed upon my spirit were the words;

"This place is a place of glory. Your human eyes are not accustomed to this glory, but as you bring your spirit into this awesome place you will begin to perceive the glory and splendour of the One whose presence fills this place. Be in awe of Him. Stand in awe of Him. Bow in awe of Him. Prostrate yourself in awe of Him. This place is all about Him, not about us. We are in awe of Him, continually, day and night. We are enthralled as we gaze upon Him. Every time we catch a glimpse of His face, especially those eyes, we are captivated. Learn to centre on Him, to be enraptured by Him who sits upon the throne, who walks among the lampstands, whose glorious and awesome presence fills this place. It is all about Him. We forget about ourselves in His presence. We have no independent existence apart from Him. We exist for Him, to stand and serve, to listen and watch, to transmit what we see and hear. For us it is all about Him and His desires and His will. We lose sight of ourselves in His awesome presence."

One of the first biblical examples of angels bringing the sense of the presence of God is during Jacob's dream at Bethel. (Exodus 28)

He dreamt of a stairway resting on the earth with its top reaching to heaven and the angels of God were ascending and descending on the stairway and God was standing at the top. When he awoke from the dream he thought;

'Surely the Lord is in this place, and I was not aware of it.' He was afraid and said, **'How awesome is this place!** *This is none other than the house of God; this is the gate of heaven.'* Genesis 28:16

The angels connected heaven and earth. They brought the sense of God's presence that was in heaven to Jacob on the earth, even in his sleep. He associated the awesomeness of the place with the presence of God. That was the place where his grandfather Abraham had raised an altar to the Lord as he journeyed through the land of his promised inheritance to mark out the territory for the Lord. He did this by erecting altars to worship the Lord throughout the land, to dedicate the land to the Lord and establish the presence of the Lord in the land God had assigned to him.[22]

God only works significantly when He is really present, therefore, the Christian goal and purpose, especially that of leaders, should be – the presence of God manifested in who or what they have been called to.

The presence of God is our priestly calling; it is to serve the presence of God, to come into His presence and receive direction in His presence. If ministry is not flowing from His presence, then it is flowing from human understanding. We may call it His presence, but sometimes His presence is not even in the place. As Revelation 3:20 shows; Jesus standing outside the Church knocking to get in!

---

22 For more details on Abraham's strategy for taking his territory and establishing an angelic presence in the land see my book, "Angels in our Territory"

Joshua's instruction to the people of Israel when they crossed the Jordan to go in and take the land was,

'Follow the ark, then you will know what way to go for you have not been this way before.' Joshua 3:3-4

The Ark of the Covenant was the place of the presence of God among his people. That was where His glory dwelt, between the cherubim. They were to be led by His glory going ahead. Similarly today we are to be led by the presence of the Lord and it is the role of angels to bring the sense of the presence of God. They live in His presence and are soaked in it. So they bring His presence to us as we draw near to Him.

Angels reveal God's Strategies

When Joshua was approaching Jericho the angel of the Lord appeared to him as a man with a drawn sword. He told Joshua that he had come as the Commander of the Lord's army. When Joshua realized who he was he fell at on the ground before him and asked, *'What message does my Lord have for his servant?'* Joshua 5:13-14 God then proceeded to give Joshua specific instructions on how to take Jericho through the Angel.

Angels are one of God's ways for revealing his strategies and directions for us to follow.

Angels fight for us and with us

When Daniel was serving God in Persia an angel came to visit him and told him that there was spiritual opposition in the heavenly realms over Persia. This high-ranking prince of Persia had opposed the angel sent to bring revelation to Daniel and delayed his arrival for three weeks. During this three-week period Daniel was fasting and praying and at the end of it the Archangel Michael came to oppose the prince of Persia and helped the revealing angel break through with his message.

The enemy opposes the work of God and this is conducted in battles going on in the <u>second heaven</u> where satan is the prince of the power of the air. We do not engage him at that level, we need to engage via the third heaven otherwise we will lose the battle and waste days if not years in prayer, praying from the wrong location.

Let me explain…

In 2 Corinthians12:1-3 Paul talks about being caught up to the <u>third heaven</u>, a place which he also describes as 'Paradise'. This is the place of God's throne and the angelic realm that John was given visions of in Revelation. It is the place that Christians are told to operate from when we draw near to God. (Hebrews 12:22-24; Colossians 3:1-4) We have been raised up and made to sit together with Christ in the heavenly realms (Ephesians 2:6) It is the place of government of the universe where all authority resides and operates from.

Satan, by contrast operates at a lower level which we refer to as the second heaven. He is described as the prince of the power of the air. (Ephesians 2:2) It is the atmosphere around the earth, the place from which he controls those who are under his authority. Some Christians mistakenly try to fight him on his ground and end up wearing themselves out in a spiritual arm wrestle with the enemy on his turf. That is not what we are called to do. Through worship in the Spirit we rise to take our places in the heavenly places 'far above all rule and authority, power and dominion, and every name that is invoked, not only in the present age but also in the one to come' (Ephesians 1:21) We lift up the name of Jesus above every other name and He despatches his troops to fight His and our enemies.

We are priests of the Most High God with access to the Holy of Holies in the third heaven. We engage in our priestly ministry of worship, prayer and fasting at the golden altar. The angel adds much incense to our prayers and presents them to God and then sends heavenly intervention through the second heaven to the earth.

Paul describes the other-worldly nature of our battles. *'For though we live in the world, we do not wage war as the world does. The weapons we fight with are not the weapons of the world. On the contrary, they have divine power to demolish strongholds. We demolish arguments and every pretension that sets itself up against the knowledge of God, and we take captive every thought to make it obedient to Christ.'* 2 Corinthians 10:3-5

On one occasion around twenty-five of us, mainly young people, were doing street evangelism in Avignon in the South of France, during the annual Arts festival. Each day we would go into the central square and stay until night, singing, testifying and preaching the Gospel. The place was crowded with all types of people from all over engaging in various forms of fringe activities and one night a group of satanists gathered around us to oppose what we were doing.

Some of them began to surreptitiously cut off pieces of hair from various team members. In removing a lock of hair, they would take it and burn it in some weird looking equipment and do a satanic ritual and incantation against the person concerned. They physically assaulted one young married man and threatened to slash open his wife's breasts. They made threats of further physical violence against us should we come out into the Square to evangelise again.

We were quite shaken by this experience as we were all young and had never experienced anything like this in the past. We came back to our premises about midnight and began to debrief. The only thing we knew to do was to pray. So, rather than go to bed we stayed up in prayer till about 4am seeking the wisdom of God.

After spending time in God's presence, someone began to confess their sin openly to the group. Then a spirit of repentance swept over the whole group. We had only been together about two weeks but people had developed little grudges against one another.

Ephesians 4:26-32 teaches us that allowing anger, bitterness, unforgiveness and other forms of sin to lurk in our hearts gives the devil a foothold in our lives and can remove our spiritual protection. We have to deal with these things if we are to have victory over the enemy in other areas of our lives and service for God.

A well-known quote is, "Keep short accounts with God!" We were to leave no ground for the enemy in our lives; these things had to be put right. So we did that.

We concluded with a time of communion as we broke bread together and remembered the covenant we had with Jesus Christ - that Jesus had defeated satan through His death and resurrection. We are in Him and share in His victory.

That night we just used the weapons of worship, repentance, communion and prayer. We didn't do much heavy intercession or fighting against principalities and powers in the second heaven. We just came to a place of oneness as a group and that was a powerful weapon against the enemy.

We decided to rest the next day and make a decision what we were going to do about the threats made against us; should we go out to evangelise again?

We concluded that we should not be intimidated by the enemy but should continue to do what God had sent us to do. As leader of the group I felt a considerable responsibility for their safety, but I knew what we had to do. So, we went out on the streets again in faith and obedience trusting God for our safety. Lo and behold, none of the satanists were to be seen, in fact we never saw them again!

I have heard of other incidents when armed terrorists have fled when attacking unarmed Christians, because they saw warrior angels coming after them. I would love to know what angelic powers had caused them to flee!

That was a very real battle which had to be fought with the spiritual weapons God has provided for us and not on the devil's terms. Sometimes he will try to lure us into battles in his territory. We have to choose which battles God wants us to fight, how, when and where. That was a turning point in our evangelism that summer. We began to see a new level of anointing on our preaching.

Normally, in the open space on the square beside all the tables with their parasols, various groups would be performing their acts, from Spanish dancers to fire-eaters. We would form a circle in the middle to sing and testify, and each group would attract people around them to watch and listen.

One day there was a heavy downpour and the various crowds ran for shelter. But the crowd listening to us stayed. One person from our spectators ran and fetched a parasol and held it over me while I preached. We experienced a new breakthrough in anointing.

In hindsight I believe the angels had come to surround us and bring the presence of God which captivated the people.

Another incident in more recent years, As I was preaching under a strong anointing, a girl in the front row drew on her tablet what she saw when I was preaching. She showed it to me afterwards and I was amazed to see that she had seen a cluster of angels tightly surrounding me as I preached. In the earlier incident in Avignon I had been unaware at the time of how the angels help us in our ministry.

Through my involvement with 'Watchmen for the Nations' in recent years I have also become more aware of certain weapons in our arsenal which have tremendous power against the enemy.

Reconciliation between various people groups who have been alienated through war and bloodshed and a history of hatred and mistrust is fundamental. I have been present in Korea and Japan at gatherings of thousands of Christians interceding for these nations. The Japanese Christians went to Korea to repent for the terrible atrocities their nation had committed against the Koreans. The Koreans forgave them, embraced them and pledged to stand together with them to see a breakthrough of the kingdom of God in the idolatrous nation of Japan. Then hundreds of Koreans went to Japan and before thousands of people proclaimed their love for the Japanese and commitment to stand with them to see a revival in Japan.

Through this reconciliation the way has been opened up for a new oneness in the body of Christ. <u>Oneness is more than unity</u>. In unity we retain our individuality as our primary identity but we harbour an attitude of love and acceptance to all other Christians. In oneness we realise that our primary identity is that we are one body, with one Lord and so we function as one in life and ministry. (Ephesians 4:4,5)

Since the charismatic renewal many began to pray for unity. But Jesus prayed for oneness – '...*that all of them may be one, Father, just as you are in me and I am in you. May they also be in us so that the world may believe that you have sent me.*' John 17:21

When nations stand together as one, genuinely bonded together by the supernatural love of God, they have great authority in prayer. This authority has devastating power against the principalities and powers in the heavenly places whose position has been sustained through centuries of idolatry.

Last year, as I was spending time with the Lord one morning, I was struck by Psalm 138:1

'I will praise you, Lord, with all my heart; **before the 'gods' I will sing your praise.***'*

Living in the Western world where idols are not overtly erected in public places, there are no temples or shrines to various gods as in Japan or in ancient Egypt. So it had never occurred to me that I should worship God before the other gods. We can worship God anywhere, but we usually think of going to church to worship God in a place set aside for that purpose. I was reflecting on this when my wife came to me and said, 'You have to go to Aswan.' At the same time as God was speaking to me through this Scripture, the Lord spoke to her by the Spirit and told her that I was to go to Aswan.

I did not know it at the time, but Aswan is a city in southern Egypt which has some of the most visited ancient idol temples in the world. So that very day I made arrangements to go to Aswan with a group of intercessors who had already planned to be there. The main god worshipped in ancient Egypt was the sun god, Ra. This is the same spiritual power behind the gods in Japan, the land of the rising sun, and in North Korea where Kim Yung-un is revered as a demi-god. The Emperor of Japan 'marries' the sun-god in a special ceremony after his accession to the throne.

In Aswan we spent three days in worship and intercession in the presence of God. There were people from thirty different nations present. We celebrated the birthday of an Egyptian pastor and prayed over him as a representative of his nation. Everyone said 'I love you' in their own language to this pastor and through him to his people. As we did this God brought about an amazing oneness in the Spirit. We pressed through to a high level of worship in the Spirit to the place where we sensed that we were at one with God. And in this oneness, we entered into a level of oneness with God and each other. Powerful prophetic intercession and declarations flowed from this place of authority, in a city where the idols had held great power for centuries.

On the second day, at one point a Japanese lady came to the piano to lead worship quite spontaneously. The Egyptians gathered around her and together these nations, where the sun god held sway, worshipped the One, True and Living God. There was a powerful time of intercession for Japan there at the stronghold and source of sun worship. The next day the Japanese showed us the photos of the biggest idol in Japan which had crashed to the ground the previous day in Okinawa, smashing its face in the steps. Kannon Sama, the goddess of mercy that people trusted in to answer their prayers, had come crashing down as we worshipped Yahweh the God of all Mercy and Grace, thousands of miles away! It was huge, about twenty-five metres high reinforced with steel bars. The Japanese don't make things to fall down! But who can resist the Lord Almighty?

We had been declaring Isaiah 19:1 *'See, the Lord rides on a swift cloud and is coming to Egypt. The idols of Egypt tremble before him.'*

As we saw these images we thought about Dagon the god of the Philistines who fell before the ark of the Lord. They put him up in his place but the next day he had fallen again and been smashed before the ark of God's presence. (1 Samuel 5:1-5)

Many of us perceive little of what is going on in the invisible spirit realm. But it is clear from Scripture that God and His celestial army of angels fight for us and with us as we learn to collaborate with him with the weapons which he has put at our disposal.

At times He sends His angels to rescue us from danger when we are serving Him. When the apostles in Acts were arrested and put in jail an angel of the Lord came during the night and opened the prison doors and brought them out with the instruction,

'Go, stand in the temple courts,' he said, *'and tell the people all about this new life.'* Acts 5:17-20

Later others were arrested by King Herod and put in prison. (Acts 12) The apostle James was put to death, and then Peter was arrested and put in prison too. But the Church prayed earnestly to God for him and God sent an angel who woke him up told him to get dressed and led him out of prison. Earnest prayer by the Church for Peter seemed to distinguish his release from James's death. Angelic activity seems to be linked to the prayer of the Church. We are told to remember those in prison as if we were their fellow prisoners. (Hebrews 13:3)

The Church is God's *'Ekklesia'*, God's governing authority in the spiritual realm. A church walking in reconciliation and oneness has authority to issue powerful spiritual decrees in prayer to effect God's government in the earth and counter the works of darkness.

The angels are actively cooperating with us in prayer, especially listening for Spirit-anointed decrees which they hear as words from the Lord. (Psalm 103:20) They then spring into activity to put into effect these decrees.

Paul was a man of continual prayer and no doubt was deeply involved in seeking God about their desperate situation when the ship he was on was in danger of shipwreck while on his journey to Rome. An angel of the Lord stood by him and assured him of his deliverance. With this angelic encouragement he was able to declare boldly to the people with him:

'Men, you should have taken my advice not to sail from Crete; then you would have spared yourselves this damage and loss. But now I urge you to keep up your courage, because not one of you will be lost; only the ship will be destroyed. Last night an angel of the God to whom I belong and whom I serve stood beside me and said, "Do not be afraid, Paul. You must stand trial before Caesar; and God has graciously given you the lives of all who sail with you." So keep up your courage, men, for I have faith in God that it will happen just as he told me.' Acts 27:21-25

Thank God for the angels He sends to rescue us when we need divine intervention. The prophet Daniel was thrown into a den of lions because of his faithfulness to serve God and defiance of the king's order not to pray to the living God. He knew what the consequences of his continued prayer would be and he was willing to face them. When the king went the next morning to the lions' den he called out to Daniel:

'Daniel, servant of the living God, has your God, whom you serve continually, been able to rescue you from the lions?' Daniel answered, 'May the king live for ever! **My God sent his angel**, *and he shut the mouths of the lions. They have not hurt me, because I was found innocent in his sight. Nor have I ever done any wrong before you, Your Majesty.'* Daniel 6:21-22

God is personally involved in sending angels to serve his servants on His assignments through them, even to fight for us as we serve Him.

The Psalmist David had called on God: *'Summon your power, God; show us your strength, our God, as you have done before…* **Rebuke the beast among the reeds**.*'* Psalm 68:28-30

Derek Kidner, in his commentary, says that this is a reference to the crocodile or to Egypt, of which the crocodile was a symbol.[23] When I was in Egypt worshipping God before the gods, we went on the Nile, which the water spirits and crocodile spirits inhabit. We worshipped Yahweh our Lord and God at the place where, in the past, a young girl would be thrown in the river every year as a sacrifice to the river gods. We did a number of prophetic acts as guided by the Holy Spirit and proclaimed our Lord to be the Lord of life.

Back home in France my wife was deeply committed to praying every day for our mission in Egypt, almost to the degree of feeling that she was there with me. One night, when she was on her own in the

---

23   188 Tyndale Old Testament Commentary on the Psalms by Derek Kidner. IVP. 1973

house, she was visited by a creature that came down the corridor to her bedroom like a water serpent 'swimming' through the air. She leapt up and rebuked the thing and told it to get out of our house. She wasn't at all afraid but was furious that this 'beast' should venture into our home and told it to go. It left immediately. Meanwhile she became aware of the presence of angels all around the house. They were on high alert and remained that way for quite some time, before resuming a more relaxed pose. As she lay in bed, every time she closed her eyes she could see angels where the ceiling was, but if she opened her eyes she saw the ceiling. She felt so peaceful under the covering of their angelic protection and fell asleep.

Angels arrange divine connections

It was an angel that appeared to Cornelius, a God-fearing man, to connect him to Peter. He had a vision and saw distinctly an angel of God who told him to send for Peter to come to him. The angel gave Cornelius the address where Peter was lodging. When Peter came and preached the Gospel the Holy Spirit fell on this household of prepared hearts and they were filled with the Holy Spirit and spoke in other tongues and were baptised. They were the first non-Jewish converts to the Christian faith and thereafter the Gospel spread rapidly to the Gentile nations. It was also an angel who connected Peter to this Gentile community. He would not normally have gone to them because of his religious bias and it took a lot of convincing to get him there.

Recently, we went for the first time to the town of Carbonne in the South of France to pray for that town. The Lord led us to return the following day and He gave my wife the commission for that day to find another Christian before we proceeded any further. Taking inspiration from the example of Peter and Cornelius we followed the leading of the Holy Spirit and we prayed that God would send an angel to guide another Christian into contact with us.

So Fran went into the streets and went up to people to ask them if they knew a Christian or a prayer group in the town. She prepared little notices to put up in shops with her contact details. Eventually a lady in the street directed her to a particular ladies' boutique where the owner knew everything about the town. So Fran explained what she was looking for and left her notice with the shop owner.

Later that day a Christian lady who was new to that area, went to Carbonne for the first time in her life and went into that same shop and began to witness to the owner and gave her a Gospel of John, having asked God to guide her that day whom she should talk to. The shop owner gave her Fran's contact details and she connected with us. Mission accomplished with supernatural guidance on both sides!

In our days many Muslims are coming to faith in Jesus Christ as Saviour. It is often through visions or dreams or angelic visitations that they are opened to meet Christ.[24]

Angels help in the ministry of healing and deliverance

I have always been a little puzzled by that enigmatic reference in the Gospel of John to an angel stirring the waters of the pool at Bethesda resulting in the healing of the first person to step into the water after the stirring.

'From time to time an angel of the Lord would come down and stir up the waters. The first one into the pool after each such disturbance would be cured of whatever disease they had.' John 5:4

Biblical commentators are quick to point out that this verse is omitted from the best manuscripts and was probably a marginal gloss to explain to readers the practice of people waiting in the colonnades at Bethesda for the moving of the waters. Whether that is true or not, it was clearly the belief of the people. Apparently the pool was fed from

---

24   'Miraculous Movements' by Jerry Trousdale, Thomas Nelson, 2012

a subterranean system and the water bubbled up from below from time to time. But people believed it was an angel although John, the author, neither endorses nor rejects that particular belief.

Bethesda means 'house of mercy' and healing is clearly an act of mercy on God's part. Healing is a big part of what God does and angels are there to serve God in all that He does.

A third of the Gospels refer to Jesus' ministry of healing and deliverance and it is a large part of what God has commissioned us to do. It is therefore no surprise that there should be healing angels who are concerned with this aspect of ministry.

Trevor Baker[25] tells of healing angels appearing at mass crusades in his ministry in India. He describes how 4000 people, mainly Hindus, came to Christ one night. He believes it was largely due to the presence of a healing angel who appeared and hovered over the crusade ground changing the whole atmosphere. God told him to say to the people, 'Bring the deaf and dumb to Me'. About a dozen came to the platform and one by one they were healed and began to speak. One little boy, deaf and dumb from birth, was carried up by his father. He turned to his father and said clearly in English, *"I love you Daddy."* The whole place erupted with excitement.

Tim Sheets[26] describes how his ministry has been transformed as he has begun to discern angelic activity in a meeting. When he discerns a healing angel beside someone he boldly declares their healing in the name of Jesus. Jesus only did what He saw the Father doing.

All we have to do is align our activity with what we perceive God to be doing by the angels He has sent.

During a week at the Melkisédek school, I taught about angels. I noticed that one of the students was somewhat handicapped. She

---

25   The Blueprints of Heaven, by Trevor Baker
26   Angel Armies, by Tim Sheets

had very limited movement in her left arm and had to use her right arm to move it. I felt challenged to pray for her healing, but I didn't know when to do so. Then, in one of the workshops, I discerned the presence of a "healing angel". So I took this as a signal to pray for her healing at that time.

She immediately began to do things that she could not do before. First she reached out her arm for the first time, and then she felt the strength coming into her fingers. During the night, she felt cracking in her fingers, and then she was able to spread them apart for the first time. Over the next few days, the healing continued. Two days later, in the next workshop, she testified what God had done and two other students continued to pray for her. Suddenly I heard cries of excitement. She had started running and jumping around the room, things that she had not been able to do before. Over the next few weeks she continued to receive prayers from different students and the healing progressed until she was able to raise her arm above her head. This is what she really wanted to be able to do as an expression of praise to the Lord. She went to see her physiotherapist afterwards and when she saw the changes, she could not give any medical explanation!

Recently, during the worship, I was about to preach when I had an image in my spirit. It was of seven angels each holding a heart between their cupped hands. I was about to preach on the supernatural life and ministry of Jesus and invite people to come to receive healing. This picture communicated to me that God wanted to heal hearts, perhaps the physical organ, or perhaps broken hearts. So after I had preached I invited people to bring their broken hurting hearts to Jesus to receive His healing power. I believe that God gives us these pictures to stir faith in the people to reach out and believe God for their healing.

Angels also collaborate with us when we are dealing directly with the enemy and taking authority in Jesus' name to drive out demons.

Sometimes in the past when we were inexperienced in the deliverance ministry, we used to have quite prolonged battles to get people free. But more recently we have realised that God's angels are there to work with us in evicting these demonic squatters. They can help in guiding us and strengthening us for quicker success in this area. We can ask the Father to send the angelic help we need for the ministry at hand.

CHAPTER 7

Angels and our inheritance

Hebrews
Chapter 1
v14; *'Are not all angels ministering spirits sent to serve those who will inherit salvation?*
Chapter 2
v1 *'We must pay the most careful attention, therefore, to what we have heard, so that we do not drift away.*
v2 *For since the message spoken through angels was binding, and every violation and disobedience received its just punishment,*
v3 *how shall we escape if we ignore so great a salvation? This salvation, which was first announced by the Lord, was confirmed to us by those who heard him.'*
v4 *God also testified to it by signs, wonders and various miracles, and by gifts of the Holy Spirit distributed according to his will.'*

I have purposely laid out the above text as it would be laid out in our Bibles. We may use different translations, but each of our Bibles are broken down into chapters and verses. But did you know the original text does not have chapters and verses? You see, chapters and verses were made by man, as a point of reference, to make it easier for you and me to find a location in Scripture. But if we are not aware of this we can miss the context. Consequently, we often lose the flow of thought which carries directly on in this instance, from chapter 1 to chapter 2.

Now let's read it as God intended without the breakdowns made by man…

'Are not all angels ministering spirits sent to serve those who will inherit salvation? We must pay the most careful attention, <u>therefore</u>, to what we have heard, so that we do not drift away. For since the message spoken through angels was binding, and every violation and disobedience received its just punishment, how shall we escape if we ignore <u>so great a salvation</u>? This salvation, which was first announced by the Lord, was confirmed to us by those who heard him. God also testified to it by signs, wonders and various miracles, and by gifts of the Holy Spirit distributed according to his will.'

The word **'therefore'** clearly refers back to the verse before. The subject of this entire passage now is clear, it is the role of angels in serving those who inherit salvation.

The Greek word *'soteria,'* which is translated here as 'salvation,' is a big word embracing the totality of the blessings Christ has acquired for us on the cross. According to Thayer, *'soteria'* includes:

A.   Deliverance, preservation and safety in the physical sphere.
B.   Salvation in a spiritual and ethical sense, as the present possession of all true Christians.
C.   Future salvation, the sum of benefits and blessings which Christians, redeemed from all earthly ills, will enjoy after the visible return of Christ from heaven in the consummated and eternal kingdom of God.

Strong's (G4990) includes health in his definition.

No wonder the writer to the Hebrews calls it ***so great a salvation*** which we must not ignore or drift away from. God wants us to enter into the fullness of all that Christ has procured for us at the cross.

Angels are assigned to serve us in our journey of laying hold of all that God has laid hold of us for. It is our responsibility to fix our eyes on the prize of the upward call of Christ on our lives, as Paul so eloquently describes.

'Not that I have already obtained all this, or have already arrived at my goal, but I press on to take hold of that for which Christ Jesus took hold of me. Brothers and sisters, I do not consider myself yet to have taken hold of it. But one thing I do: forgetting what is behind and straining towards what is ahead, **I press on towards the goal to win the prize for which God has called me heavenwards** *in Christ Jesus.'* Philippians 3:12-14

There is a dimension of this great salvation which Paul is already living in, but there are further aspects of his inheritance that he has yet to lay hold of while still in this life. But it is only in the life to come that we enter into the fullness of our inheritance. Peter says:

'Praise be to the God and Father of our Lord Jesus Christ! In his great mercy he has given us new birth into a living hope through the resurrection of Jesus Christ from the dead, and into **an inheritance that can never perish***, spoil or fade.* **This inheritance is kept in heaven for you***, who* <u>*through faith are shielded by God's power*</u> *until the coming of* **the salvation that is ready to be revealed in the last time.** *'* 1 Peter 1:3-5

Peter refers to the new birth which has already been given to those who are born-again through faith in the blood of Jesus. That new birth includes a living hope of a future inheritance for us in heaven which satan cannot touch. As we walk in faith we are shielded by God's power and His ministering angels until they are sent to gather the elect from the four winds and usher us into the final phase of this great salvation.

'Then will appear the sign of the Son of Man in heaven. And then all the peoples of the earth will mourn when they see the Son of Man coming on

*the clouds of heaven, with power and great glory. And **he will send his
angels with a loud trumpet call**, and they will gather his elect from the
four winds, from one end of the heavens to the other.'* Matthew 24:30-31

But until then, there is a temporal inheritance that God has for us in
this life. It is a clear goal towards which God has called us.

The children of Israel had been delivered from Egypt and entered
into a blood covenant relationship with God. But their inheritance
was never in the wilderness, although many mourned and died there.
There was a land flowing with milk and honey which God had
prepared for them and for which He had saved them. They had to
believe God and press through the wilderness till they reached their
promised land. Then they had to take possession of it stage by stage,
until they were enjoying the fullness of God's provision for them.

To help them to reach their destiny and enter into their inheritance,
God promised angelic help, guidance, and protection. This was part
of the covenant promises God had made to them.

*'See, **I am sending an angel ahead of you** to guard you along the way
and **to bring you to the place I have prepared.** Pay attention to him
and listen to what he says. Do not rebel against him; he will not forgive
your rebellion, since my Name is in him. If you listen carefully to what
he says and do all that I say, I will be an enemy to your enemies and will
oppose those who oppose you. My angel will go ahead of you and bring you
into the land...'* Exodus 23:20-23

Blood Covenant Promises

The concept of a blood covenant is central to the Bible. God enters
into relationship with His people through covenant.

The covenant God made with Abraham was the foundation of two subsequent covenants: the Old Covenant (or Mosaic Covenant) and the New Covenant made through the blood of Jesus.

God took the initiative with Abraham and made an unconditional covenant which He unilaterally ratified by walking through the severed sacrifice as a smoking fire pot and flaming torch. (a theophany, Genesis 15:17)

He made covenantal promises to Abraham concerning an heir and an inheritance. He would give him a son, a numerous posterity and a land – a specified territory as an eternal inheritance.

Abraham's part was to believe God and he did so, and was credited with righteousness for his faith. He thus became the father of faith with both natural descendance who were to inherit the land of Israel, and spiritual descendance who were to inherit the world.

*'It was not through the law that Abraham and his offspring received the promise that he would be **heir of the world**, but through the righteousness that comes by faith.'* Romans 4:13

The Mosaic covenant, or Old Covenant, is described in the Book of the Covenant. (Exodus chapters 20-23) This was a covenant between God and the redeemed people of Israel. God gave them stipulations of how He expected them to live if they were to be faithful to this covenant – the Ten Commandments, given at the beginning of the Book of the Law. He concluded the Book of the Law by giving ten promises at the end of chapter 23:20-33.

These promises were conditional on the people observing the Ten Commandments. The people ratified this covenant with God declaring, *'Everything the Lord has said we will do.'* Exodus 24:3 They sealed the covenant by taking the blood of young bulls; they sprinkled half of it on the altar and half of it on the people signifying God's agreement and the people's agreement. Done deal!

'Moses took half of the blood and put it in bowls, and the other half he splashed against the altar. Then he took the Book of the Covenant and read it to the people. They responded, 'We will do everything the Lord has said; we will obey.' Moses then took the blood, sprinkled it on the people and said, 'This is the blood of the covenant that the Lord has made with you in accordance with all these words.' Exodus 24 :6-8

We are familiar with the Ten Commandments, (or the Ten Words as they were known to the Jews), but we are less familiar with the ten promises, so let us look at them.

1.   *An angel to lead us into our inheritance. (v20,23)*
2.   *A covenant partnership with God against our enemies. (v22)*
3.   *God's blessing on our food and water. (v25)*
4.   *Removal of sickness from our midst. (v25)*
5.   *No miscarriages. (v26)*
6.   *No barrenness. (v26)*
7.   *A full life span. (v26)*
8.   *Victory over all our enemies. (v27)*
9.   *The full possession of our entire inheritance, eventually. (v28-30)*
10. *Secure established boundaries. (v31)*

These promises reveal the heart of God for his covenant people. The New Covenant is described in Hebrews as a better covenant with better promises. And Paul affirms,

'For no matter how many promises God has made, they are 'Yes' in Christ. And so through him the 'Amen' is spoken by us to the glory of God.' 2 Corinthians 1:20

This gives us some idea of the areas of life where God has an inheritance for us. But often, like the children of Israel entering the

Promised Land, we have to fight through doubt and fear to lay hold of our inheritance.

God had told them that He had given them the land, but they had to go and take possession of it, in faith and obedience. Only when they obeyed and followed the strategy God gave them for each situation did they find that angelic help was released to them and victory was realised.

In most of these ten areas, we too have our battles to fight. Walking in faith and in obedience to God are the twin conditions for the covenantal blessings to be released.

Several years after God had made the covenant with Abraham there was still no sign of any of the promised blessings. God appeared to him again to affirm His side of the covenant and to remind Abraham of his part.

*When Abram was ninety-nine years old, the Lord appeared to him and said, 'I am God Almighty; **walk before me faithfully and be blameless.** Then I will make my covenant between me and you and will greatly increase your numbers.'* Genesis 17:1-2

Abraham was to walk before God, not before men. The Hebrew word for *'blameless'* can be rendered *'upright'*. He was to walk in faith and integrity. Abraham, the great man of faith certainly had several lapses and acted out of fear when he lied about Sarah in order to save his own skin, and twice at that!

God had chosen Abraham to direct his children after Him to keep the way of the Lord, by doing what is right and just.

*'For I have chosen him, so that he will direct his children and his household after him to keep the way of the Lord by doing what is right and just, **so***

***that** the Lord will bring about for Abraham what he has promised him.'*
Genesis 18:19

In order to bring up his children to do what is right and just, Abraham
needed to set the example himself. Perhaps God was just giving him
a gentle reminder of his covenantal obligations before fulfilling the
promises. Likewise, the promises of the Old Covenant, established
under Moses, were based on a walk of integrity in obedience to the
Lord. And under the New Covenant we too are also reminded of this
correlation when we examine ourselves at communion.

Removal of Sickness

Some people say that it is all down to faith. If we are not healed it
is because we don't have enough faith! Others are quick, like Job's
comforters, to say that it is because of sin in our lives that we are
not healed. Certainly, either may be the case, as 1 Corinthians 11
makes clear. But it is also true that neither may be the case! But at the
same time we need to recognise that a walk of faith and obedience is
foundational to our covenantal relationship with God. Some place
an imbalanced emphasis on grace that causes people to live carelessly
rather than *'perfecting holiness out of reverence for God.'* 2 Corinthians
7:1 In any case it is helpful to ask God to show us the reason for
delayed fulfilment and what our strategy should be.

In one situation God had been asking me for some time to do a forty
day fast and I was prevaricating. Then one day when I bent down to
pick up the phone a disc in my back went out. I was reduced to lying
on the flat of my back by such a simple act. I had plenty of time to
consider my ways. So when the elders came to pray for me I knew
what I needed to confess and put right.

*'Is anyone among you ill? Let them call the elders of the church to pray
over them and anoint them with oil in the name of the Lord. And the*

prayer offered in faith will make the sick person well; the Lord will raise them up. If they have sinned, they will be forgiven. Therefore confess your sins to each other and pray for each other so that you may be healed. The prayer of a righteous person is powerful and effective.' James 5:14

I was brought up in a church where that passage was quoted in part, and no reference made to confession. There is a biblical injunction here and Paul makes clear that weakness, sickness or premature death may be caused by lack of faithfulness to our covenant obligations to our Lord. (1 Corinthians 11:27-33) James however is careful to put a proviso, *if they have sinned*, implying that that may not necessarily be the case.

Sometimes sickness is an attack of the devil to be resisted and fought off with the weapons God has given us.

On another occasion that was definitely the case for me. I had had a history of haemorrhages from duodenal ulcers over a number of years. But God had healed me and I was trouble-free for quite some time. Then one night, after we had begun a church-planting project in a new area, I had a sudden attack. I had all the usual symptoms of an impending haemorrhage (I'd had 16 previously, so I knew them well). I was lying and writhing on the floor of our living room and I called Fran to come and pray for me. My wife is like a spiritual '*battle-axe*', because she really knows how to battle in prayer and take on the enemy. She battled and prayed in tongues and in English until she broke through and all the symptoms disappeared and I was able to get up and go to bed and sleep. Sometimes the devil wants to discourage us or hinder us in God's work and sickness is one of the weapons he uses.

No Miscarriages

Ignorance of God's promises can rob us of the blessings God wants to give us. On one occasion my wife had a miscarriage and we lost our preborn baby. At that time I was ignorant about the promise of no miscarriages in Exodus 23. But several years later, Fran had all the same symptoms of an impending miscarriage. This time we knew the promise and set about the battle to claim the promise and fight for the life of the little one she was carrying. I sat on the bed beside her and laid hands on her tummy and, under the anointing of the Spirit, prophesied over the life of the boy she was carrying. The symptoms disappeared and she finished her pregnancy normally and gave birth to a healthy boy. We called him Daniel, meaning God is my Vindicator, and he has been such a blessing, bringing much joy to us.

No Barrenness and Premature Death

Many people have to battle with sterility. For Abraham and Sarah it took twenty-five years for that curse to be broken. Abraham's son, Isaac, and his wife Rebekah were barren for twenty years, but Isaac prayed for his wife and God gave her twins. We have not personally had a problem with sterility, but sterility has been in my family line in each of the generations that I know about. Sometimes that can be the result of generational iniquity through occult involvement or curses for various reasons. We have not yet seen this broken (at the time of writing) but are praying for breakthrough.

We have, however, seen breakthrough in the lives of others. A young lady in our church was told by the doctor that she would never be able to have a baby because of endometriosis. But God gave Fran a *'word of knowledge'* that she would have a baby. She prayed for her and she gave birth to a healthy baby who is now a young man with an anointing to lead worship. More recently, a neighbour who was unable to have any children came to ask us to pray for her. God gave me a verse from the Bible, *'He settles the childless woman in her home as a happy mother of children. Praise the Lord.'* Psalms 113:9 We kept claiming and declaring that verse. She now has beautiful twin girls! We prayed for another couple who were longing for a child but were unable to have one. Even after prayer things didn't change immediately and they planned to try fertility treatment. But before going out the door to get the treatment, they said 'Let's do the pregnancy test one more time!' Lo and behold she was pregnant and now they are rejoicing in a beautiful daughter.

God wants us to enjoy a full life span. A dear lifelong friend of mine, when in his twenties, had a fear of premature death. He used to have dreams, or rather nightmares, about dying. But God has set him free from these fears and he is now in his seventies and going strong.

Ministry Inheritance

Every believer has a ministry... can I get you to read that again... **every believer has a ministry and that includes you!** You see, we can limit God, by thinking that unless we are in so-called 'full time ministry', or on a platform, we do not have a ministry. This is not true! We each have a destiny which God has planned for us before we were born. God said to Jeremiah,

'Before I formed you in the womb I knew you, before you were born I set you apart; I appointed you as a prophet to the nations.' Jeremiah 1:5

It wasn't just before Jeremiah was born; it was even earlier. It was before he was formed in the womb. God knew his spirit person before his conception and the beginning of the formation process of his body. God sent Jeremiah's spirit into the womb to be knit together with his forming body in the mystery of life.

'For you created my inmost being (spirit); you knit me together (spirit and body) in my mother's womb. I praise you because I am fearfully and wonderfully made; your works are wonderful, I know that full well. My frame was not hidden from you when I was made in the secret place, when I was woven together in the depths of the earth. Your eyes saw my

unformed body; all the days ordained for me were written in your book before one of them came to be.' Psalm 139:13-16

The same is true for each of us. God sent us into this world for a purpose. He had a destiny in mind for us. He even had a book written containing His plans for our lives before we lived a single day.

The devil wants to rob us of our destiny. He doesn't want us to enter into and take possession of the territory God has assigned to us - our ministry inheritance.

Our specific territory is the sphere of life God wants us to impact for the kingdom of God. Many Christians fail to lay hold of their inheritance in this life, just like the first generation of the children of Israel who failed to enter the Promised Land, because of their unbelief. The devil wants to keep us wandering in the wilderness with a limited level of experience with God, much less than God has for us. The Israelites experienced manna for forty years yet all the time God had a land flowing with milk and honey waiting for them to possess. We can settle for a manna equivalent in our day, when in fact God has so much more for us. Angels are there to help us to inherit al that God has planned for us.

Gideon's inheritance

Gideon lived at a time after the children of Israel had entered their inheritance, but they were not living in the good of it. They were not walking in faithfulness to their covenant with God and for seven years the Lord let the Midianites oppress them. They were living in caves and clefts in the mountains and temporary shelters in the land God had given to them, because of their disobedience and idolatry.

Like others, Gideon would thresh his wheat secretly for fear of the Midianites who would steal their crops and leave them impoverished.

Then one day an angel appeared to Gideon and sat down under an oak and began talking to Gideon. He began by saying, *'The Lord is with you mighty warrior!'* The angel knew that Gideon's destiny was to be a mighty warrior and he had come to speak prophetically over him declaring God's purpose for his life. He wasn't living in his destiny.

He wasn't possessing his inheritance. So the Lord, through the angel, commissioned him, *'Go in the strength you have and save Israel out of Midian's hand. Am I not sending you?'* Judges 6:14

Gideon, like so many of us, began to make excuses and plead weakness and powerlessness. So God had to reassure him that He would be with him and he would be successful in delivering Israel from Midian. Gideon prepared an offering for him and the angel added some 'special effects' in a rather cool 'disappearing act'.

'The angel of God said to him, 'Take the meat and the unleavened bread, place them on this rock, and pour out the broth.' And Gideon did so. Then the angel of the Lord touched the meat and the unleavened bread with the tip of the staff that was in his hand. Fire flared from the rock, consuming the meat and the bread. And the angel of the Lord disappeared.' Judges 6:20-21

However, Gideon was not yet equipped to take on the Midianites while there were false gods in his own household. So, God instructed him to tear down his father's altar to Baal and cut down the Asherah pole and build a proper altar to the Lord in its place. Gideon was afraid to do it in the sight of his family and the men of the town, so he did it at night. But even with fear he did it! In the end when the men of the town challenged Gideon's father over his son's actions, his father defended him. The very act had obviously freed him from the power of Baal. He said, *'If Baal really is a god, he can defend himself when someone breaks down his altar.'* Judges 6:31

Only after Gideon had dealt with idolatry in his family did the Spirit of the Lord come upon him powerfully to deliver Israel from the Midianites in quite a dramatic fashion.

There are often spiritual reasons why we are not entering into our destiny. Sometimes there is generational iniquity in our family line that needs to be dealt with. Dealing with iniquity in our generational line is a priority for breakthrough into the fullness of our inheritance.[27]

One of the things that God has brought to light to my wife has been witchcraft and Freemasonry in her family line. These things bring many curses on subsequent generations. Scripture makes it clear that we need to confess our own sins and the sins of our fathers and renounce their wicked ways if we are to enter into the fullness of our salvation/deliverance and have the curses broken. (Nehemiah 1:4-11) Only then can we enter into the fullness of our inheritance. Nehemiah understood that the reason for Israel's exile and the loss of their inheritance was due to the sins of idolatry of repeated generations. That had to be dealt with before full restoration could take place.

We see in the opening chapters of Zechariah the prominent role the angels had in the process of restoration of Israel's inheritance. The angel that appeared to Gideon clearly knew God's destiny for his life and had a clear role in helping him towards that destiny.

This is one of their very specific purposes in our lives. I believe that not only do we have a guardian angel assigned to us from birth, but that when God sets us apart for our ministry, he assigns angels to work with us to lead us into our inheritance. We have to listen and cooperate or we may fall short of God's best for us.

Angelic prompting

On one occasion when I was just becoming aware of angels and their

---

27 'Repentance, Cleansing Your Generational Bloodline' by Natasha Grbich.

ministry to me, I was going for a walk along the promenade by the sea. For the first time I had the faint sense that a couple of angels were following me. When we came to a bend I turned left as I usually did when going on this particular walk. As I did so I had the sense, albeit faint, that the angels had gone straight ahead and that they had stopped to look around and see if I was going to follow them. I shrugged the prompting off as if it were just my imagination and kept going my own way.

A little bit farther along a naked woman appeared on the beach in a display of full-frontal nudity. It wasn't even summer time and it was not a nudist beach. That was not what I needed in my pursuit of walking with God! The devil clearly used it to distract my mind, even though I had strenuously sought to avoid pornography on the internet. It took me quite some time to get that image erased from my mind and concentrate on purity of vision. If I had heeded the angels' gentle prompting I would have avoided that. I later went back to that spot and got down on my knees and repented. Sometimes it may be a very still small voice, but we need to tune in to it and be sensitive to its prompting. As Scripture states... '*Whether you turn to the right or to the left, your ears will hear a voice behind you, saying, 'This is the way; walk in it.'* Isaiah 30:21

Angelic guidance to the place God has prepared

The first of the ten promises God gave to Israel was of an angel to go before them to protect them on the way and to bring them to the place which God had prepared for them. But they had to listen to him and obey him because he spoke on God's behalf. This was the promise God gave to us when he called us to France. And we have been so blessed to see the practical ways the angel has gone ahead of us and brought us to the place God had prepared for us at this season of life.

Before moving to Toulouse we had visited a couple of times to search out the area we would like to live in, but no rental properties meeting our criteria were available. The various estate agents took our details and promised to let us know if something became available. We kept looking on the internet during the three months before we were due to move but still nothing.

Eventually we packed our car and left Ireland without having found a place. We went in faith believing that as God had promised, He would send an angel ahead of us to lead us to the place he had prepared. We were at peace and not at all anxious, just excited to see how God would work it out. We later were told that there are 25,000 people who move to Toulouse every year as it is a thriving city, capital of the aeronautical and aerospace industries in France and Europe. Consequently, accommodation is very difficult to come by.

We arrived late on Saturday night, stayed in a hotel overnight and went to church on Sunday. Sunday evening we checked the relevant websites again and still there was nothing suitable. On Monday morning we went out to visit the same estate agents again, but each time there was nothing meeting our criteria. When we had finished all the ones we knew, we unexpectedly found one we had not seen previously. After taking our details he informed us that a new house had just come in and he hadn't yet got it advertised. He took us to see it. My wife said 'I like it' and that was all I needed to hear! We took it! In one morning with angel help we got what three months on the internet couldn't provide. We were later told repeatedly, 'That never happens!' But God had sent his angel ahead as He had promised to prepare a house for us to live in.

We are excited to see the goodness of God and see how God is giving us new spheres of ministry even in our senior years! I encourage you to lay hold of whatever God has written in His book for your life. Ask Him to show you and lead you into the territory He has for you to inherit.

"Angels are our fellow servants."

CHAPTER 8

Partnering with Angels

In their book, *'Angelic Encounters'* James and Michal Ann Goll quote an encounter Rolland Smith had with angels. In this encounter Rolland Smith records that one of the angels said to him, *"The church on earth does not know or seem to care to understand what the invisible armies in heaven are doing. They are very preoccupied with their celebrations and feasts... When the church comprehends what we are doing and is ready to fight together with us in complete obedience to our glorious Head, Jesus Christ, then we will win the war".*

That is a clarion call to the Church to understand what the invisible angelic armies are doing and then to collaborate with them to see the invisible armies of darkness vanquished and the kingdom of God manifested in fullness on the earth.

The Bible doesn't talk about co-operating with angels. But it does say we are God's co-workers. (1 Corinthians 3:9) The Greek word is *'sunergos'* which means a 'companion in work or fellow-worker.' (Thayer's Greek Lexicon) It is similar to the word 'fellow-servant', which the angel used in describing his relationship with the apostle John. (Revelation 19:10; 22:9)

This time the Greek word is *'sundoulos'* which Thayer defines as ''a fellow servant, one who serves the same master with another.' (Thayer's Greek Lexicon)

So, as servants of the Lord, we are serving God together with the angels, working together to serve the same master, collaborating whether or not we are consciously aware of it in any given situation. The angels seem to be more aware of this than we are, as it was the angel who informed the apostle John about their collaborative role. We are on this same team and any team works better when we understand how to work together.

Understand the role of angels

Firstly, it helps to understand the role and function of angels in God's plan. That's why most of this book is about explaining what the Scriptures teach us about their role, illustrating it with biblical and personal examples.

In any team it is important that each player knows clearly what the coach is expecting of him, but each player also needs to know the role of the other players around him. Each needs to know where his responsibilities begin and end. When he has played his move, he needs to pass the ball to the next player. If he overplays when he should pass, the team is less effective. In the army of God the terrestrial army needs to know when to move to best collaborate with the celestial army.

A good example of this is when David was fighting the Philistines.

*'Once more the Philistines came up and spread out in the Valley of Rephaim; so David enquired of the Lord, and he answered, 'Do not go straight up, but circle round behind them and attack them in front of the poplar trees. **As soon as you hear the sound of marching in the tops of the poplar trees, move quickly**, because that will mean the Lord has gone out in front of you to strike the Philistine army.' So David did as the Lord commanded him, and he struck down the Philistines all the way from Gibeon to Gezer.'* 2 Samuel 5:22-25

God gave David the signal when it was time to move, to attain maximum effect because the angelic army had gone ahead to do their part. Spiritual sensitivity and timing are important in discerning the moment. Usually, God gives us an advance sense of what He is doing and then an impulse from the Spirit comes to move us to action at the right time.

Develop the gift of discernment of spirits

One of the most unused gifts in the Church and yet one of the most valuable ones is the gift of discernment of spirits.

The various gifts of the Spirit are usually given to enhance our ministry in response to our earnest desire. Any new gift is like learning a new language, it takes time and plenty of practice, listening to the voice of the Holy Spirit. It also helps if we are in an environment where this is nurtured and practised. 'Iron sharpens iron' so we can learn from and support each other. Being part of a prophetic community helps us to sharpen each other and raise our expectations and experience.

We must be sure we don't operate from wrong motives that can derail what God had intended for good, or with hardness of heart which can block our spiritual discernment.

Like Balaam, even though he was a prophet, did not see the angel that was blocking his path, when his donkey did, God was angry with Balaam and sent an angel to oppose him. (Numbers 22:21-35) His heart was not right and his motives were wrong. Outwardly he prophesied accurately that God's blessing was on Israel and he could not curse them, as Balak wanted him to do. But surreptitiously he counselled Balak to entice Israel to sin by inviting them to their idol sacrifices where their women seduced the men to indulge in sexual immorality. (Revelation 2:14)

There was no sorcery or divination that could be effective against Israel the people of God but the sins of idolatry and immorality removed their divine protection and exposed them to satan's attacks. (Numbers 23:23) A plague broke out against them and 24,000 died as a result, until Phinehas the priest intervened and the plague was stopped. Their angelic protection was removed through sin, and the prophet's discernment was lost through sinful greedy motives.

Live in complete obedience to God

We must obey the Word of God and be actively involved in the mission God has given us. The children of Israel did not experience the presence and activity of the angel that God had promised when they disobeyed and refused to go into the Promised Land. It was only when the subsequent generation obeyed and crossed over the Jordan that they discovered that the angel of the Lord was ahead of them with instructions for the next phase. We need to go in obedience and faith that angelic help is there, because often we do not see them or even perceive them.

We should also obey any directives we get from an angel of God. *'Pay attention to him and listen to what he says. Do not rebel against him; he will not forgive your rebellion, since my Name is in him.'* Exodus 23:21

Mary submitted to the word of the angel, the shepherds did so too, and Zechariah eventually believed and obeyed. He discovered the consequences of not believing when he was struck dumb!

Recognise our need of angels and ask God for their help

We need to recognise our need of angels and ask God to send them to help us. Jesus said that He could have asked the Father to send legions of angels to rescue Him from the cross, but He knew that was not the Father's plan. He may well have asked for angelic help in Gethsemane when He felt overwhelmed by the power of darkness.

The writer to the Hebrews tells us in 5:7:

'During the days of Jesus' life on earth, he offered up prayers and petitions with fervent cries and tears to the one who could save him from death, and he was heard because of his reverent submission.'

On several occasions the Jews had tried to put Jesus to death prematurely and Jesus had escaped because it was not His time. He knew he had the authority to ask his Father for angelic help and God heard him when he did so.

On one occasion Fran and I were driving across England to catch the ferry to Ireland from Liverpool. We thought we had left plenty of time for the overnight journey but we had not counted on extensive road works on the motorway. The ferry was due to leave at 3am and we arrived at the edge of Liverpool about 2.45am wondering if we would make it in time. Then our SatNav took us to the wrong ferry terminal and there were no signs to the terminal for Dublin. So I thought, *"Lord this would be a good time to send an angel."*

Amazingly, we found the right way to the right terminal without signs or SatNav, but it was then 3am and the gates were shut. There was no one at the ticket booth. We could see the ferry loading some final vehicles, so I got out and rattled the gate to try and draw attention. No response. We were getting quite desperate as we had driven a long way from France through England and wanted to get home to Ireland. The thought of spending another twenty-four hours waiting for the next ferry didn't bear consideration. Then another car drove up and a lady got out and told us to go to the HGV entrance and we would be admitted. I felt like asking her 'Are you an angel?' It turned out it was another passenger who had arrived before us and found out what to do and then came back to tell us! Or was she really an angel? She was certainly an answer to our prayers for angelic help, whether human or divine.

Become aware of their presence and activity

When we enter into a purposeful time of worship, it draws in the worshippers of heaven who are the angels. As they arrive, we sense an increased intensity of God's presence. While keeping our focus on God, we can also tune in to what is happening in his entourage. It is usually the angels that communicate that intensified sense of God's presence. We may automatically be aware of what they are doing or we can ask God to show us what they are doing.

Observing what the angels are doing can give us the direction in which to lead the meeting. And if the angels are celebrating joyfully then we will want to join with them in that joyful celebration. If healing angels are present, we will want to cooperate with them and invite people for healing.

Some people have even seen angels with spare body parts. When they have announced this, people who needed healing have experienced creative miracles.

When beginning our prayer around Occitanie I sensed angels trumpeting '*Prepare the way of the Lord.*' That was the cue for us to collaborate in declaring what they were declaring. At the end of our prayer tour, as we crossed the boundary of the territory to re-enter for our return journey, we sensed a welcome party by the angels of that territory. They were rejoicing and singing. We likewise experienced an incredible sense of joy and celebration. We sang and rejoiced with the angels in a way that we had never done before. We sang exultantly the Christmas carol:

> "*Sing, choirs of angels, Sing in exultation;*
> *Sing, all ye citizens of heaven above!*
> *Glory to God, in the highest,*
> *O come let us adore him, Christ the Lord!*'

We were like David calling on the angels to praise God.

*'**Praise the Lord, you his angels**, you mighty ones who do his bidding, who obey his word. **Praise the Lord, all his heavenly hosts**, you his servants who do his will. Praise the Lord, all his works everywhere in his dominion. Praise the Lord, my soul.'* Psalm 103:20-22

It was an incredible time of collaborating in joyful celebration with the angels at the conclusion of a mission God had given us to do, and when we became aware of their activity, we joined in.

Do prophetic actions

Prophetic actions are a powerful spiritual weapon for pulling down spiritual strongholds.

'The weapons we fight with are not the weapons of the world. On the contrary, they have divine power to demolish strongholds. We demolish arguments and every pretension that sets itself up against the knowledge of God, and we take captive every thought to make it obedient to Christ.' 2 Corinthians 10:4-5

The Greek word here translated *'arguments'* is *'logismos'*, which means 'a reasoning.' (Strong G3053)

An altar to the 'goddess Reason' was erected in Notre Dame Cathedral in Paris at the French revolution. This is a major spiritual stronghold throughout the Western world, especially in France. It influences the minds of the whole Western civilisation whether or not one is aware of it. It elevates human reason to a position of supremacy in people's lives rather than the human spirit.

Reason has its proper place in our lives, but it should not have the place of supremacy. For the Christian it is the quickened spirit which should have the supremacy.

You may have heard the expression, "body, soul and spirit!" which is used quite often even in churches. But Scripture tells us in 1 Thessalonians 5:23 that we are *spirit, soul and body*, and remember it is in that order, therefore the spirit should be in the place of supremacy with our reason in subordination to it.

Our soul consists of our mind, will and emotions. Our spirit is joined to the Holy Spirit at new birth and made one with Christ. (1 Corinthians 6:17) Our soul is being sanctified through the ongoing work of the Holy Spirit to conform us to the likeness of Christ. (Romans 8:29) Hence our thinking needs to be aligned with God's thinking through the Spirit and the Word. That is a process that is not yet complete, so our mind or reason should not have the highest place in the process of guidance. The Holy Spirit communicates with our human spirit which in turn communicates with our mind so that we know and understand God's will. (1 Corinthians 2:10-16) We do not abandon the use of our reason as some do; we just keep it subordinate to our spirit and aligned to the Word.

Prophetic acts do not make sense to the human mind. For example, marching around Jericho for seven days and then shouting on the seventh day doesn't make sense as a military strategy. But it was a prophetic act which God told them to do. When they did so, God's celestial army was activated to knock those walls down. Likewise, Elisha told King Jehoash to open a window and shoot an arrow and declare: *'The Lord's arrow of victory, the arrow of victory over Aram!'*

It was not a logical action to the human mind, but it was a prophetic act declaring in the spirit realm, *'You will completely destroy the Arameans at Aphek.'* 2 Kings 13:15-17

When God told us to drive in stakes with four declarations written on them, around the region of Occitanie, it didn't make sense to the rational mind. But it was a spiritual act of obedience to the Lord to take the territory for Him. When we encircled it in prayer, one of our intercessors in Ireland saw the territory surrounded with angels as we did so.

Prophetic acts operate in the spirit realm and bypass the human mind because we are listening to the Spirit rather than reason. But until we learn not to put our trust into the arm of the flesh we will really battle with reason at times in order to obey.

Align our proclamations with the decrees of God

The angels are listening for the Word of God in order to spring into action to execute it. (Psalm 103:20) When we pray, it is good to pray God's Word. Prayers of proclamation are effective prayers. They are prophetic and powerful.

'As the heavens are higher than the earth, so are my ways higher than your ways and my thoughts than your thoughts. As the rain and the snow come down from heaven, and do not return to it without watering the earth and making it bud and flourish, so that it yields seed for the sower and bread for the eater, **so is my word that goes out from my mouth: it will not return to me empty, but will accomplish what I desire and achieve the purpose for which I sent it.** *'* Isaiah 55:9-11

I grew up hearing that passage quoted in the context of preaching. But now I see it more in the context of praying prayers that begin in heaven and pass through our mouths to go back to heaven. It is compared to the evaporation cycle in nature, where rain and snow come down from the clouds and make the earth fruitful, then are returned to the clouds by evaporation to continue the cycle.

In our praying we need to be listening to God, in the Spirit and in the Word. When God gives us a declaration that comes from His mouth and we align our proclamations with God's Word, the angels are activated to execute it. We don't make decrees willy-nilly out of our own heads. We decree what God gives us to decree and it is that which has authority in the spirit realm.

Activating Angelic Activity

I have to say here, for a long time I didn't understand that we have an active role in releasing angels to do their work in our sphere. Like many Christians, I was totally passive in relation to any involvement with angels. I assumed that, since it was God who sent them, He would do that whenever He wanted without any need for involvement on my part. If He sent them, well and good, if not that was ok also. He is sovereign and can do whatever He wishes in the spiritual realm.

However I had learned that in other aspects of ministry, for example in relation to spiritual gifts, while on the one hand God gives the gifts sovereignly as His Spirit wills (1 Corinthians 12:11), on the other hand He tells us to eagerly desire spiritual gifts (1 Corinthians 14:1), and that God gives to those who ask, seek, and knock at his door persistently. (Luke 11:9-12)

For example, a man who had been many years in ministry came to see me one day desperate to speak in tongues. Until this time, he had always had the attitude that if God wants to give him tongues, well and good, but if not then that was ok too. It was up to God, in his opinion. But he had reached a point in his life and ministry where he was facing such pressures he realized that he needed to be able to pray in the Spirit with other tongues in order to get breakthrough. I recognized that he fulfilled the biblical conditions of being thirsty for the Spirit and eagerly desiring the gift of tongues, so I laid hands on him and immediately he began to speak in a real flow of the Spirit in languages he had never learned. In fact, after leaving me he continued to speak in tongues for about two hours in the car. God is sovereign but he seeks our active collaboration with him.

I began to sense in my spirit that the angels were waiting for us to invite them and release them to operate within my sphere of ministry. I was still rather unsure biblically if it was right for me to do so. But in one meeting the speaker, after his message, asked me to come to the microphone and release the angels to minister. When I did so, my wife said afterwards that that was the most anointed part of the meeting. Immediately there was the sense of God at work.

On another occasion when I was teaching on the ministry of angels I felt I should actively release the angels to do their ministry. So, I said, "I release the angels in this meeting to fulfil the mission and mandate God has sent them for in this gathering." Almost immediately I began to sense angelic activity and perceive an angel or angels with someone for a specific purpose. As I began to share what I was sensing, people began to respond and confirm what I was sharing.

In one case I saw a group of angels closely grouped around one young lady. I asked God to show me why they were there and what their assignment was. He showed me it was to give her favour with people of influence and to open doors for her to usher her into the presence of influential people in the secular realm, where she was to have an influence for the kingdom. Also, she was going to be a speaker with presence and authority. She confirmed to me afterwards that that had been prophesied to her previously and she was believing for that to take place. She found real encouragement from receiving that confirmation to press on into what God had for her in spite of past difficulties affecting her ability to speak with confidence.

Together with my wife, I began to do activation workshops regarding the gift of discernment of spirits, particularly in the context of discerning angelic presence and activity. I began to pray like Elisha for his servant, "Lord open our eyes to see what you want to show us in the spirit realm. Show us what you are doing with your angels so that we may collaborate with you. Keep us from seeing what you don't want us to see."

I discovered that, when we did this, other people began to share what God was showing them and we began to pray into that for their lives to line up with what God was doing.

I remember Bill Johnson sharing that God often teaches us through a miracle rather than through theology. Our theology teaches us to understand how God works before we experience it. So we do lots of practical training as well as teaching in the hope that we will begin to experience the truth learnt. This is often true with the realm of healing. But God doesn't need our theology conditioned by Western rationalism in order to act. He can act and then afterwards give us understanding that lines up with His worldview.

When I was entering into these new experiences with angelic activation, I was waiting on God one day still trying to understand from a biblical perspective my role in releasing the angels to do their activity. Like a flash of light, I suddenly felt God showing me that the angels came to serve me in my sphere of authority and anointing.

'The highest heavens belong to the Lord, but the earth he has given to the human race.' Psalm 115:16

God gave man authority in the Earth realm. It is our sphere of authority. He gave Adam authority to exercise dominion and fill the Earth and subdue it. Even when he fell God did not withdraw that mandate. Jesus came as man to redeem the Earth for men and when He had done so He said, *'All authority in heaven and on earth has been given unto me. Go therefore and make disciples of all nations...'* Matthew 28:19-20. (2 Corinthians 10:13) This may be a geographical sphere or territory or a particular type of ministry sphere. But we have authority in the sphere on Earth that God has assigned to us. Angels recognise authority and operate directly under God's authority since they are sent by Him on their assignments. But they also recognise His delegated authority to us and are here to serve us in the sphere of our authority. So we have authority to release them to fulfil their divine mandate in our sphere of authority and ministry.

I felt that this revelation gave me a biblical understanding so that I can operate with greater confidence, boldness and faith in releasing angelic activity in the future. We have a clear role in collaborating with God as his co-labourers. A large part of our ministry involves the authority of the spoken Word. That is how God operates His authority. He speaks and things happen, because His created universe responds to the authority of His spoken Word.

In sending us with His authority, Jesus made demons and sickness subject to our authority (Matthew 10:1) and He promised to be with us confirming His word with signs following. Paul made clear that God assigns to each person their sphere of authority.

Our ministry is to proclaim the Gospel and speak forth the Word of God, to speak healing and command deliverance to the captives. Demons understand and respond to our authority. They also know when we are trying to operate outside of our sphere of authority.

So we need this clear biblical understanding of our authority in relation to angels. I do not believe that it is an authority to command angels, because only God has that authority. But it is an authority to release them to operate and do what God has sent them to do, within our sphere of authority and ministry.

"Angels are sent to receive us at death and accompany us to heaven."

CHAPTER 9

Angels and death

We prefer not to think about death or talk about it; so many people do not prepare adequately for it and don't know how to face it when it comes. One American doctor was present at the harrowing death of a terrified patient. On coming out afterwards he met the pastor and said to him, 'I wish you pastors would teach your people how to die!'

Jesus taught us about death and about the role of angels at our death. He told the story in Luke 16 of the rich man and Lazarus both of whom died but with contrasting outcomes.

Lazarus was a poor beggar but he clearly had a faith in God, for when he died he was carried by the angels to Paradise where he was with Abraham the father of faith. The rich man died and was buried and found himself in hell as he had made no spiritual preparation for the afterlife.

'Precious in the sight of the Lord is the death of his faithful servants.'
Psalm 116:15

God highly values the moment His faithful children transition from this life to the next. He sends His angels to accompany them so that they have no fear going through the valley of death. They are His welcome party sent to usher them into the presence of God. It is a glorious moment!

God sent a chariot of fire and horsemen of fire for Elijah, that faithful prophet, when the time came for him to go. (2 Kings 2:11) The angels were going to bring him to heaven in style!

Of course there are many premature deaths in tragic circumstances that cause much grieving for loved ones. But there is also the undeniable truth that if they were born again and walking with God, they have entered into the better life of the age to come.

At the tender age of six my father came face to face with the death of his father. When his father knew he was dying, he brought in each of his children personally to share some last words with them.

He said to my Dad, 'Willie, I'll meet you at the pearly gates.' My father never forgot those words. Years later, when he was eighteen, the brakes on his bicycle failed going down a steep hill. At the bottom of the hill there was a T-junction and a car ran over him. They pulled him out from under the car not expecting him to be alive. But he got up, put his crumpled bike over his shoulder and walked back up the hill home. He told his mother he didn't feel too well and went to lie down. She didn't know what had happened till the police arrived to follow up on the accident.

He realised what a narrow escape he had had and then he remembered his father's last words to him and realized that had he been killed, he wasn't ready to meet his dad at 'the pearly gates'. So he went to a Gospel meeting and gave his life to the Lord. Over seventy years later my two brothers and I were with him as he peacefully went to meet the Lord after a full life and, indeed, was ready to be re-united with his father.

My father had twin sisters who were less than two years old when their dad passed away. Ten years later, at the age of twelve, one of them took a terminal illness. When she was approaching the end she asked the family who were with her, 'How will I know that I am about to die?' They replied, 'You'll see the angels coming for you!' A short time later she suddenly sat up and excitedly said, 'There they are now!' And then she dropped back onto the bed and into the angels' arms, to be carried to her heavenly Father, and her earthly one whom she had never really known. What a comfort at the difficult time of death to know that our heavenly Father sends a personally assigned angelic party to accompany us into His presence.

Fran and I have lost two grandchildren as babies. One only lived two hours and the other three months. Their loss has been a great grief to their parents and to us. One day when my wife and I were praying with a friend of ours, who had tragically lost her son in a cruel accident, my wife suddenly had a vision. She saw a doorway open in heaven and our two grandchildren were standing there the older one holding the younger one by the hand. They waved at her, and as the door began to close they said 'Goodbye Grandma'. What a reassurance to know that our little ones who die are carried safely to heaven's shore to await our arrival there too!

In Ireland, and indeed elsewhere, there are many superstitions or misunderstandings about what happens when a baby dies. I once heard a priest say to the parents of a child who had passed away, 'Don't pray for him, pray to him!' The implication was that somehow the child was now in a position to hear and answer their prayers and grant them favours. Completely unbiblical! I have heard others say 'He's now a star up in the sky!' or 'He's now an angel'! None of these things are true according to the Scripture. We don't take our theology from 'The Lion King,' or any other story from mythology. For those who die and know the Lord, including children who are too young to understand, their human spirit goes to heaven to await the return of Christ and the resurrection when they will receive glorified bodies free from sickness or disability or mortality.

Jesus said that they are '**like** the angels in heaven', not that they become angels. (Mark 12:25)

The status of Christians in heaven is higher than angels whereas on earth it is lower than angels. Referring to the creation of mankind the Psalmist says in 8:6:

'What is mankind that you are mindful of them, human beings that you care for them? You have made them a little lower than the angels and crowned them with glory and honour. You made them rulers over the works of your hands; you put everything under their feet.'

In the order of creation man is lower than the angels, but in the order of grace he is given the role of ruling over the angels. Paul said to the Corinthian believers: *'Don't you know that we will judge angels?'* 1 Corinthians 6:3 Our glorified position is that we will rule with Christ over all God's creation. (Revelation 22:5)

Death is but the portal through which we enter a new and better life for all eternity. When angels are sent to receive us at death and transport us to heaven.

A bright yellow light

In 2016 the news headlines were about a fifteen-year-old girl who died in an aeroplane at Nice airport in France after an allergic reaction to a Prêt à Manger sandwich. Natasha had severe food allergies from childhood and had to be very careful about what she ate. Both she and her father read very carefully the labelling on the sandwich they bought at the airport in England before flying to their holiday home in France. They were both satisfied that, according to the label, it contained nothing for her to worry about.

About twenty minutes into the flight she became unwell and took some antihistamine medication. But her body came out in red swollen welts and she began to have difficulty breathing. Her father gave her an adrenalin injection in the aeroplane toilet. But she still couldn't breathe and said "Daddy help me!" She asked for another adrenalin injection but within a minute she was falling over. They called a stewardess and gave her oxygen but she went totally unconscious. There was a newly qualified doctor on the flight and they laid her out on the galley floor; then she went into cardiac arrest.

When the plane landed at Nice airport, five paramedics came straight on and tried CPR. Her heart came back after forty-five minutes but stopped again then returned faintly then disappeared.

Meanwhile the pilot and some of the cabin crew were crying. Just then, her father saw five angels floating around over Natasha's body. They were human like figures but with wings on their backs.

They radiated a strong soft yellow light, intense and soothing, glowing but not hard on the eyes. Her father lifted his arm and wished them away saying "It's not her time!" They left and Natasha died. He now realises that they had come on a mission to take Natasha's soul to heaven.

Natasha's father, Nadim Edam-Laperouse, was a successful British businessman and an atheist. He had been awarded an MBE at Buckingham Palace for services to business, had shared a platform with the prime minister and was a confident self-made man. His father was from Afghanistan and his mother, from France, and they were totally non-religious. He saw no functional need for a god. But in that unimaginable situation of watching his daughter die he felt totally helpless.

Natasha had started going to church about a year previously and only recently had asked to get baptised. Nadim had never gone to church except once for a funeral. They brought Natasha's body home and went to her church and have been going since. One day at work when he felt like crying, he went down to the basement floor where it was dark.

Suddenly that same bright yellow light appeared and lit up the area. He realised that God had come to comfort and strengthen him. Throughout the five-day inquest he would go to the toilet and pray for God to bring to the light what the various companies wanted kept hidden. And it happened. Subsequently he has been successful in seeing legislation brought in to change food labelling laws. He has done a lot of media interviews since Natasha's death but had not previously spoken about seeing angels.

But on Christmas eve 2019, three years after the event, he gave a full interview to the BBC with the above account. He wanted to tell in a truthful way, without embellishment, what really happened so that others could hear it. He and his wife, Tanya, know that Natasha was taken to heaven by angels, and they now know that they will be with her when the time comes.[28]

---

28   BBC Radio 4, 24th December 2019, A bright Yellow Light.

"Angels will be part of the glory move coming that will impact the whole of mankind!"

CHAPTER 10

Angels and the glory

The seraphim are a particular rank of angel that are associated with the presence and glory of God. Isaiah had a vision in which he saw the Lord exalted upon his throne with seraphim above him.

'In the year that King Uzziah died, I saw the Lord, high and exalted, seated on a throne; and the train of his robe filled the temple. Above him were seraphim, each with six wings: with two wings they covered their faces, with two they covered their feet, and with two they were flying. And they were calling to one another: 'Holy, holy, holy is the Lord Almighty; the whole earth is full of his glory.' At the sound of their voices the doorposts and thresholds shook and the temple was filled with smoke.' Isaiah 6:1-4

A seraph is a winged angel with a fiery appearance. Their role is to worship God, proclaiming His holiness and His glory in all the earth. The sound of their voices shook the door frames of the temple and shook Isaiah to the core. It was a life-transforming experience which propelled him into one of the most significant prophetic ministries the world has seen.

Angels, who dwell in the glory of God in heaven, bring his glory to earth to impact our lives. This happened to the shepherds.

'The angel of the Lord appeared to them and the glory of the Lord shone around them, and they were terrified.' Luke 2:10

Scripture repeatedly affirms that God's purpose for the world is that the earth will be filled with his glory as the waters cover the sea. (Habakkuk 2:14)

This will involve much angelic activity as the servants of his glory. They worship the God of glory in the heavenly realm and minister His glory in the Earth realm.

The Elijah ministry of the end times is to *prepare the way for the Lord... and the glory of the Lord will be revealed, and all mankind will see it.* Isaiah 40:3-5 There is a movement of glory coming that will impact the whole of mankind. Elijah's ministry on Earth ended in a moment of glory when a chariot of fire and horses of fire appeared, and he went up into heaven in a whirlwind.

'He makes his angels winds and his servants a flame of fire.' Hebrews 1:7 quoting Psalm 104:4

He sends his angels to take all of us, His children, to be with Him when the time has come for us to go. He certainly did it in style for the specially anointed prophet!

Elijah appeared in glory with Jesus on the mount of transfiguration with Moses who had also experienced the glory on Mount Sinai. Elijah had called down fire to consume the sacrifice as the glory of the God of Israel was revealed in contrast to the powerlessness of Baal. We can expect some powerful end-time glory confrontations as we approach the culmination of human history and we prepare for the King to return in his glory.

*'When the Son of Man comes **in his glory**, and **all the angels** with him, he will sit on his glorious throne.'* Matthew 25:31

What a glorious consummation to human history when all of heaven's angels accompany Jesus on his glorious return to set up his kingdom on Earth!

I believe we are fast approaching the return of our Lord in glory. The signs of His coming, as Jesus described them, are increasingly manifest and yet we can be lulled into indifference by the daily round of life, work, pleasure, and leisure. We have the Elijah mission *'to prepare the way of the Lord'* and to gather in the final harvest before the King of kings returns. May we deny ourselves, take up our cross and follow Him in this mission. And He will send all the angelic help we need.

BIBLIOGRAPHY

The Unseen Realm, Michael Heiser, *Lexham Press, 2015*

Thayer's Greek Lexicon of the New Testament

Strong's Exhaustive Concordance online

Le Réveil des Cevennes, Pierre Demaude, *Editions Réveille-toi, 2015*

The Gifts of the Spirit, Derek Prince, *Whitaker House: 2007*

The Seer, James Goll, *Destiny Image Publishers, 2012*

Psalms 1-72, Derek Kidner, *Tyndale Old Testament Commentaries, IVP: 1972*

Miraculous Movements, Jerry Trousdale, *Thomas Nelson, 2012*

The Blueprints of Heaven, Trevor Baker, *River Publishing: 2012*

Angel Armies, Tim Sheets, *Destiny Image Publishers, 2016*

Angels in our Territory, Graeme Wylie, *Maurice Wylie Media, (Updated) 2020*

Repentance, cleansing your generational bloodline, Natasha Grbich, *House of Ariel Gate, 2009*

Contact

To contact the author, see:
facebook.com/territorialangels

Or email:
info.harvestfrance@gmail.com

To order *Angels in our Territory*:
www.harvestfrance.com

Also available in French:
«Les anges dans notre territoire»

www.laboitechretienne.com

Lookout for Graeme's next book

"The Companion Volume"

Inspired to write a book?

Contact

Maurice Wylie Media
Inspirational Christian Publisher

Based in Northern Ireland and distributing around the world.

www.MauriceWylieMedia.com